BUILDING BRIDGES
WITH
BILINGUAL BOOKS
AND
MULTICULTURAL RESOURCES

BUILDING BRIDGES

WITH

BILINGUAL BOOKS

AND

MULTICULTURAL RESOURCES

A Practical Manual of Lesson Plans, Literacy Games,
and Fun Activities from Around the World
to Celebrate Diversity in the Classroom and at Home

Anneke Vanmarcke Forzani

with

Dr. Heather Leaman, Edmond Gubbins, Ellen O'Regan

Language Lizard
Basking Ridge

Building Bridges with Bilingual Books and Multicultural Resources
Copyright © 2019 Anneke V. Forzani
Published by Language Lizard
Basking Ridge, NJ 07920
info@LanguageLizard.com   www.LanguageLizard.com
Telephone 888-554-9273

Notice: The information in this book is true and complete to the best of our knowledge. It is offered without guarantee on the part of the author or Language Lizard. The author and Language Lizard disclaim all liability in connection with the use of this book.

Library of Congress Control Number: 2019919035

ISBN: 978-1-951787-00-4 (Print)
ISBN: 978-1-951787-01-1 (Ebook)

To my children and the leaders of tomorrow -
young people who show courage, grace, and tolerance
even in the face of adversity.

BOOK BONUS

More Multicultural Lesson Plans and Free Diversity Resources!

Save time with free educational content! Download additional multicultural lesson plans and exclusive bonuses at **www.LanguageLizard.com/Bonus**.

You will receive:

- A colorful downloadable "HELLO" chart
- "I'm Bilingual, What's Your Superpower?" activity sheet
- "Celebrating the Bilingual Child Month" - teacher suggestions handout
- A special discount on the multicultural/bilingual books featured in the lesson plans in this book.

There are many additional multicultural lesson plans available on the Language Lizard site and we continue to add more each year. Subjects include:

- Understanding and Appreciating Cultural Differences
- Cultures and Folklore (includes Mexican/Hispanic, Native American, Chinese folklore)
- Building Community in the Classroom
- Language, Customs, and Culture (lessons on India, Korea, Japan, Romania)
- Appreciating Diverse Cultures and Religions
- Countries, Food, and Culture (focus on Morocco, Poland, Mexico)
- Supporting our Classmates: Folktales, Bullying, and Problem Solving
- Happiness (Social & Emotional Well-being)

Subscribe to our newsletter to be notified when new lesson plans are available! www.LanguageLizard.com/Newsletter

PRAISE FOR *BUILDING BRIDGES*

"This is an amazing resource! I love the lesson plans. They are ready to use and the inclusion of parent letters is a wonderful idea. The games are a great idea. My students will love them. This book will be so useful to so many!"

Caia Schlessinger, *President of NJTESOL/NJBE, ESL Teacher*

"An incredible and much-needed resource for educators and home school families. With easy to use lesson plans and activities to teach children about other languages and cultures. For over 15 years Anneke Forzani has been instilling the skills and understanding needed to foster global citizenry in our children. *Building Bridges* is a must-have for every home, school, and library. Planting the seeds of courage, grace, and tolerance in our multicultural and diverse world."

Valarie Budayr, *Co-Founder of Multicultural Children's Book Day*

"*Building Bridges* is an excellently structured, comprehensive, and exciting resource, guaranteed to help foster inclusion and a sense of community while simultaneously creating enjoyable learning experiences for children. The lesson plans, in addition to the vast bank of games and activities, are of brilliant use to teachers for literacy development and social studies learning. In addition, the book helps foster meaningful links between school and home life, enabling parents to play an active role in their child's education. At a time when our society is rapidly diversifying, I commend Anneke Forzani's efforts in creating this superb book that enables partners in education to confront and positively deal with these societal changes."

Maire Garry, *Elementary School Teacher*

"*Building Bridges* is a tremendous resource that is practical and contains relevant literacy lessons rooted in best practice. The background information section of the lesson plans provides preservice teachers with essential knowledge and materials important for lesson implementation. Additionally, the procedures are clearly written and easy to follow with strategically placed leveled questions. I particularly like the section on current research supporting the use of dual language books so preservice teachers can truly understand its value and place in the classroom. *Building Bridges* is invaluable for any classroom."

Lisa Gordon, *Adjunct Professor, Department of Literacy, West Chester University*

"As a homeschooling mom, I am always searching for ways to incorporate fun methods to encourage learning. As a bilingual mom, I aim to introduce this way of learning in two different languages. . . . and expose my children to different cultures. *Building Bridges* offers valuable tools to help me accomplish these goals in an informal, organic way. I am grateful to have found this resource as our bold task is now more easily attainable."

Ana Skaarup, *Homeschooling Parent*

"This book is a great resource to have in any classroom! The snapshots of the lessons make it easier for teachers to find what they are looking for, whether they are using this text as a resource or just looking for a lesson. Lessons are well outlined and user friendly. I love that the lessons include hands on activities and games for kids to enjoy while learning about diversity, ethnicity, and culture. This text is a great resource promoting multiculturalism with many selections of games, books, and activities to help immigrant kids to feel more accepted and understood.

Melissa Manrique, *English as a Second Language Specialist*

"Teachers can use this book as a resource for incorporating more multicultural resources for students of different cultures and backgrounds to create a welcoming environment. The lesson plans are beyond useful in helping teachers cultivate a culturally responsive classroom while demonstrating awareness for students' differences. Materials that are provided help alleviate the extra work that may appear daunting to some teachers, so this resource will encourage more teachers to implement cultural diversity in their teaching."

Paige Dea, *Kindergarten Teacher*

"A wonderful and important resource providing teachers and families with practical guidance to cultivate children's understanding and appreciation of diverse languages, cultures, and ethnicity. This book creates positive links with dual-language and minority children that are essential to forming a welcoming and inclusive environment. The wealth of easy-to-follow, fun activities create a variety of opportunities for meaningful conversations about multiculturalism. This book is a celebration of diversity in a global age."

Laura Harrison, *Elementary School Teacher*

"*Building Bridges* is not only an invaluable tool for any teacher working in a diverse classroom, but also a timely resource for every single educator amidst times of growing intolerance and prejudice. . . . *Building Bridges* is not limited to the lesson plans which are outlined in great detail within, but rather offers templates, activities, and games which can be effectively implemented in any context."

Seán Gleasure, *Primary School Teacher*

"This is an outstanding book that helps teachers strive to be culturally responsive. This resource book contains numerous activities and lesson plans that are adaptable for any age and ability level. Exposure and understanding of other cultures is a critical component in school today as the world grows ever more connected."

Katie Rodgers, *Middle School Teacher*

"Teachers and homeschoolers who are seeking ways to add diversity including foreign languages and culture into their curriculum, now have a wonderful new resource. This new book is a practical hands-on resource of lesson plans, games, activities, and bilingual books for kids."

Mia Wenjen, *Co-founder of Multicultural Children's Book Day*

TABLE OF CONTENTS

Table of Contents

ACKNOWLEDGEMENTS

Over the past 15 years I have had the privilege of working with many dedicated teachers who are committed to building welcoming classrooms for all children. Their feedback, input, and ideas enhanced this book in countless ways. It has been a pleasure supporting these educators, and I am grateful for their ongoing efforts advocating for immigrants and refugee children. I also thank Dr. Heather Leaman, Edmond Gubbins, and Ellen O'Regan for their invaluable support and practical knowledge of the challenges faced by teachers, ensuring that the multicultural lesson plans are effective in diverse classrooms not just in the United States, but globally. Thanks to Sue Kwon, Corey Heller, and Justin Gelish for their creative input, and to Diane Costa and Suzanne Skalski for their astute reading and editing of this book.

I am grateful to my parents, Erik and Margaret Vanmarcke, who immigrated to the U.S. and experienced both the challenges and rewards of the "American dream." They ignited my love of languages and cultures, and always encouraged me to follow my passions. I thank my children, Tommy, Joey, William, and Christopher, for their love and laughter, for encouraging me to brave new challenges, and for keeping me young at heart. Interacting with their generation gives me great hope for the future. I am also eternally grateful to my husband, Ed Forzani. His encouragement and support made the experience of building Language Lizard and writing this book, while raising a family, infinitely more enjoyable.

INTRODUCTION

*Could a greater miracle take place than for us to look
through each other's eyes for an instant?*
- Henry David Thoreau

The Purpose of this Book

Our communities have become increasingly ethnically, linguistically, and culturally diverse. Approximately 27 percent of the overall United States population is made up of immigrants and their U.S. born children. The foreign-born immigrant share of the total U.S. population has risen from 4.7% in 1970 to about 13.5% in 2016, and includes increasing numbers of residents from Latin America and Asia.

Schools are filled with bilingual children who speak numerous languages at home. In 2016, over one in 5 children in the U.S. spoke a language other than English at home. The percentage of children who do not speak English at home varies widely by state, from a low of 2% in West Virginia to a high of 44% in California.

While Spanish is the most prevalent non-English language spoken in the U.S., other common languages spoken at home include Chinese, Tagalog (Filipino), Vietnamese, French, Arabic, Korean, Russian, and German. The rich linguistic diversity includes over 350 languages, with great variation by region.

While the majority of immigrants speak English proficiently, about half of the foreign born population is Limited English Proficient (LEP). Although the numbers of LEP students vary by region, schools everywhere are working hard to adequately support these students.

Unfortunately, many new arrivals, as well as students in established minority communities, are dealing with various forms of discrimination. At the same time, their teachers, many of whom were not specially trained to teach in such diverse settings, are struggling to support these students and meet the needs of their increasingly diverse student body. Schools are looking at ways to increase parental involvement among immigrant communities, while immigrant families are trying to stay connected to their culture and language. In addition, many educators and homeschooling families have recognized the importance of teaching children about diverse cultures and languages to help them succeed as global citizens.

It is in this context that I began working with Dr. Heather Leaman, Professor of Education in the Department of Early & Middle Grades Education at West Chester University in

Pennsylvania, to develop this resource. Our aim is to support the educational experience of young children by providing a practical resource for teachers and families to promote multiculturalism and build inclusive classrooms.

The purpose of this book is to provide an actionable, easy-to-use resource for educators and homeschooling families to teach children about other languages and cultures while supporting literacy development and multiculturalism. To that end, this book offers *multicultural lesson plans*, *diversity activities*, *games*, and *other resources* that educators can use to:

- build inclusive and welcoming classrooms,
- develop self-esteem among minority children,
- promote an overall understanding of and respect for diversity, and
- support literacy development in multiple languages.

With the resources in this book, we hope educators find it easier to respond to the needs of the multicultural classroom while at the same time meeting federal and state teaching requirements.

Most of the activities and lesson plans in this book apply to elementary and preschool classrooms or homeschooling environments. The lesson plans use multicultural books that are available with bilingual text in English and a choice of many different languages. This provides educators with the opportunity to incorporate books in various languages and represent diverse communities in their classrooms.

It should be noted that many of the issues associated with integrating and educating immigrant families and language learners require important policy changes and affect resource allocation. Such policy changes are essential, and we refer to some excellent resources for those who have the ability to affect this change. Yet reviewing those policy issues in detail is beyond the scope of this book.

Why We Created this Resource

Since founding Language Lizard in 2005, I have had the privilege of working with teachers and literacy organizations that support the educational and social development of immigrants, refugees, and dual language learners. I also work with teachers who were accustomed to more homogeneous student bodies, but whose classrooms have become increasingly diverse. These educators make great efforts to find appropriate resources to meet the needs of their students. Similarly, I continue to support numerous immigrant families who struggle to maintain their family's culture and home language.

Dr. Leaman works with pre-service teachers focusing on social studies in the elementary grades. She also works with practicing teachers in the Master's of Education program at West Chester University, and coordinates their M.Ed in Applied Studies in Teaching and Learning, supporting teachers as they conduct classroom-based research. While interacting with these teachers, she has seen firsthand the need for resources that support their efforts to successfully teach in diverse classrooms.

In 2006, Dr. Leaman and I began working together with her students to create lesson plans using dual language books as a way to help new teachers increase their understanding of work with bilingual learners and linguistically diverse families. We developed a series of multicultural lesson plans that were offered as a free resource on the Language Lizard website (www.languagelizard.com). We found that bilingual books were an excellent resource for introducing languages and cultures to children. As teachers used the books and lesson plans to introduce cultures, holidays, and languages of the minority children to the rest of the class, the children felt recognized and included. It helped to boost their self-esteem and pride in their unique heritage. Similarly, the non-minority children developed a greater understanding and appreciation of the "differences" of their classmates.

Over the years, I have spoken with teachers and families about how they have used these multicultural lessons and bilingual books. I have used their feedback to develop ideas and suggestions that can make multicultural learning fun, improve literacy, and enhance parental involvement in education.

After seeing how well our multicultural lesson plans were received, and reviewing the trove of ideas developed over the years, I decided to embark on this book. My aim was to develop an easy-to-use resource that would help teachers and families to develop inclusive multicultural classrooms and homes. At the suggestion of Dr. Leaman, I was extremely fortunate to have the help of two wonderful teachers from Ireland, Edmond Gubbins and Ellen O'Regan. Having completed their Bachelor of Education degrees at Mary Immaculate College in Limerick, Ireland, they are both elementary school teachers who work with students from Pre-Kindergarten to sixth-grade in Ireland. They received scholarships to undertake their Master's of Education in Applied Studies in Teaching and Learning at West Chester University in Pennsylvania, which led to their involvement in this project. I am indebted to them for the great contribution they made in developing the creative and comprehensive lesson plans in this book.

What You Will Find in this Book

This book includes numerous ideas and resources to help educators teach students about other cultures and languages. Although some of the activities are best for classroom settings, many can be adapted for use in homeschooling environments or recommended to families who are trying to maintain a heritage language. Readers can skim the resources in the table of contents and then easily reference the sections that are most helpful at any particular time.

Before delving into the specific lessons and activities, we take a look at data that highlights the increasing diversity in our communities. We also briefly address some of the challenges faced by immigrants, establishing why it is so important to build multicultural classrooms and how this book can be used to respond to the issue.

We then move into the "meat" of the book: a set of comprehensive multicultural lesson plans that fit into three major themes:

1. **Cultural Awareness and Diversity**: To provide children with tools that allow them to become aware of cultural diversity and foster relationships based on respect, equality, and diversity.

2. **Folktales, Fables, Myths, and Legends**: To expose students to a range of traditional literature from different cultures and countries, enabling them to appreciate the multitude of stories told to children around the world.

3. **Holidays/Festivals**: To provide children with opportunities to learn about and appreciate a range of holidays and festivals from around the world.

These lesson plans use some of our favorite bilingual books to explore these three themes. All of the bilingual books profiled in the lesson plans are available in a choice of many languages (with English), so teachers have an opportunity to incorporate the languages of students in the classrooms into their lessons, and even engage parents who speak those languages. Some sections of the lesson plans can also be taught without the featured books.

In the next section of the book, we outline numerous cultural diversity activities that we have provided over the years to immigrant families and teachers in multicultural classrooms. These activities will promote a greater understanding of and appreciation for diversity overall, while also helping children with diverse backgrounds feel more welcome and proud of their heritage. Many of the activities offer ways to engage parents from diverse backgrounds.

This is by no means an exhaustive list. Rather, these are simple ideas that educators can pull from and build on to teach children about other languages and cultures. This section includes:

- Ways to use bilingual books to improve literacy and support language awareness.
- Sample games, crafts, and foods from other parts of the world to expand a child's worldview.

- Interesting information about languages to help students begin to appreciate linguistic differences.
- Unique holidays and events that can be used as a springboard to promote multiculturalism and literacy.

Finally, we provide additional resources (and links) that teachers can reference in their efforts to build multicultural classrooms, promote parental involvement, and support immigrants and refugees. This section also includes some "extras" including a colorful chart that can be used to immediately welcome children in many languages.

BACKGROUND DATA & CHALLENGES

If man is to survive, he will have learned to take a delight in the essential differences between men and between cultures. He will learn that differences in ideas and attitudes are a delight, part of life's exciting variety, not something to fear.
– Gene Roddenberry

In this section, we first paint a broad picture of diversity in the United States. We look at how trends in immigration have changed over time and review statistics about immigrant children. We share data on overall language diversity and English proficiency, including a look at some state data.

We then raise issues surrounding discrimination in schools. We provide examples and suggestions on ways to address some of these challenges. All of this provides a basis for why we wrote this book and why it is important to build multicultural classrooms.

The Data: Increasing Ethnic and Linguistic Diversity

Note: The data presented in this book focuses on the United States. It is pulled from U.S. Census Bureau data, including the 2016 American Community Surveys (ACS) and the 2017 Current Population Survey (CPS). That said, readers in Canada, Europe, and other areas of the world are experiencing similar trends in immigration and increases in diversity.

The U.S. is also not alone in experiencing an increase in nationalism and its impact on discrimination against refugees and immigrants. As such, the ideas and lesson plans presented in this book are useful to any community with a culturally and linguistically diverse population.

Those interested in immigration trends of the twenty countries or areas hosting the largest numbers of international migrants may visit the following link on the United Nations website: http://www.un.org/en/development/desa/population/index.shtml.

Overall Immigration Changes

We are living and working in increasingly diverse communities. According to the 2017 Current Population Survey (CPS), about 27% of the overall U.S. population is made up of immigrants and their U.S. born children (approximately 86.4 million people).

While the overall percentage of foreign-born immigrants has fluctuated over time, there has been a steady increase since the Immigration Act of 1965, which abolished national-origin admission quotas. Foreign-born immigrant share of the total U.S. Population has risen from about 4.7% (9.6 million people) in 1970 to 13.5% (43.7 million people) in 2016. The majority of immigrants are naturalized citizens, lawful permanent residents, and legal residents on temporary visas.

The 1960s brought the highest immigration from Italy, Germany, and Canada, whereas the late 20th and early 21st centuries saw many more immigrants coming from Latin American and Asian countries. In 2016, roughly 26% of immigrants were from Mexico. Indians, Chinese (including Hong Kong but not Taiwan), and Filipinos made up another

15%. Other countries in the top 10 included El Salvador, Vietnam, Cuba, the Dominican Republic, South Korea, and Guatemala.

Children of Immigrant Parents

There were about 70 million children under the age of 18 living in the U.S. in 2016. 18 million of those children (26%) lived with at least one immigrant parent. 2.1 million were born outside the U.S., while the remaining 15.9 million were second-generation children who were born in the U.S. to at least one foreign-born parent.

The percent of all children in the U.S. living with immigrant parents increased from about 13% of all children in 1990 to 26% in 2016. That said, the number of second-generation children has grown since 1990, while the number of foreign-born children has declined since 2000. So overall, the trend shows that a growing percentage of children in immigrant households are born in the U.S. (from 77% in 1990 to 88% in 2016).

While states such as California, Nevada, New Jersey, New York, and Texas have the highest share of children living with immigrant parents, other states are seeing particularly high percentage growth. Tennessee, Kentucky, Delaware, Alabama, and the Carolinas showed the highest percentage growth of children of immigrants from 2000 to 2016.

Of children in immigrant families, about 14% have difficulty speaking English and about 55% live with parents who have difficulty speaking English. About 21% live in a "linguistically isolated household" (ie. no person 14 years or over speaks English "very well").

Language Diversity

With the diversity in immigration comes greater language diversity as well. In 2016, about 22% of the U.S. population ages 5 and older reported speaking a language other than English at home. This is almost a three-fold increase since 1980. Among children 8 and under in the U.S., almost one third are growing up in households where at least one parent speaks a language other than English.

Spanish was by far the most common of the non-English languages spoken at home. Other top languages with *approximate* percentages are listed below:

Percentage of those 5 and older who reported speaking a language other than English at home (2016):

Spanish (or Spanish Creole): 62%
Chinese (includes Mandarin and
   Cantonese): 5%
Tagalog: 3%
Vietnamese: 2%
Arabic: 2%
French (including Cajun): 2%
Korean: 2%
Russian: 1%

German: 1%
Haitian Creole: 1%
Hindi: 1%
Portuguese: 1%
Italian: 1%
Polish: 1%
Amharic/Somali/other Afro-Asiatic
   languages: 1%

Although this list shows the most common languages other than English spoken at home, there are over 350 languages spoken in communities around the country. This includes languages such as Nepali, Sgaw Karen, Chaldean, and Burmese, which are some of the more common languages spoken by refugees (along with Arabic and Somali), according to the U.S. State Department's Refugee Processing Center.

English Proficiency

Most U.S. residents who speak another language at home are also proficient in English. However, about 26.1 million U.S. residents ages 5 and older, approximately 9% of the U.S. population, are Limited English Proficient (LEP). This represents a considerable increase since 1990, when the LEP share of the total U.S. population was about 14 million (6% of the population). LEP means that they report speaking English "not at all," "not well," or "well" on the survey. To be considered proficient, they must report speaking English "very well" or speaking English only.

The states with the highest share of LEP residents in 2015 are as follows:

California: 19%
Texas: 14%
New York: 14%
Hawaii: 12%
Nevada: 12%
New Jersey: 12%

Florida: 12%
Massachusetts: 9%
Illinois: 9%
Arizona: 9%
New Mexico: 9%

Some areas have particularly high representation of LEP residents, with certain counties in Texas, Alaska, and Florida having more than a third of its population aged 5 and older classified as LEP. As expected, the languages spoken vary dramatically across the country based on where certain communities have migrated over time.

Close to 80% of the LEP population spoke Spanish, Chinese, Vietnamese, Korean, and Tagalog. Although Spanish continues to be the most common language spoken in the homes of English language learners (ELL), a language other than Spanish was the top language in 5 states. For example, Somali was a top language spoken by ELLs in Maine, whereas a high percent of ELLs in Vermont spoke Nepali. In Alaska and Hawaii, many ELLs speak indigenous languages such as Ilokano and Yupik. (*Note: state ELL data from the U.S. Department of Education's "SY 2012-13 Consolidated State Performance Reports."*)

As we consider linguistic diversity, it should be noted that many of the top languages spoken by ELLs are *not* based on the Latin alphabet.

A Key Challenge:
Combating Discrimination
in Schools

Along with the increase in diversity in schools, there has been considerable discrimination towards minority students and families. The rise in nationalism in many countries, together with empowered anti-immigrant groups, has led to numerous hate crimes, outright racism, and discrimination against minorities. While this discrimination has increased the challenges and struggles of children in immigrant communities, there are more subtle forms of discrimination apparent in schools that are worth discussing as well.

In September 2015, the Migration Policy Institute (MPI) published a report that examined the types of discrimination among children of immigrant families, and the negative impact of that discrimination on their school experiences: *The Impact of Discrimination on the Early Schooling Experiences of Children from Immigrant Families* by Jennifer Keys Adair.

The MPI report reviews both personal and structural discrimination that exists against children of immigrants. Personal discrimination pertains to the way they are treated and the kinds of learning experiences that schools offer them. Structural discrimination refers to "long-term institutional practices that affect their personal development and academic trajectories."

Many of the report's recommendations for alleviating some forms of both personal and structural discrimination are geared toward policymakers and go well beyond the scope of this book. For readers involved in developing educational policy and determining financial resource allocations, I highly recommend reading the report in detail. That said, the report does address a number of strategies that can be acted upon by educators in day-to-day classroom activities to alleviate some forms of discrimination and enhance the educational experience of immigrant children. It is these issues that I highlight in this section and which are addressed in the strategies and lesson plans presented in this book.

For example, one of the personal forms of discrimination presented in the report is the **devaluation of primary languages**. Some educators, rather than supporting bilingualism, devalue students' home language skills. According to Dr. Adair, "they may view the ability to switch between English and Spanish as a problem to be fixed rather than a skill to be developed. Instead of building on children's multiple, complex language and cultural skills, educators often attempt to acculturate them away from home languages and cultures. Studies have shown that strong ties to families and co-ethnic communities support learning, while alienation from them inhibits cognitive and socioemotional development."

Another personal form of discrimination faced by children of immigrants relates to **negative interactions** with other students and adults. For instance, a peer might point out how a minority child looks or sounds different, or ask why their parents don't speak English well. Similarly, immigrant children may overhear racist comments or criticism of their culture or their parents. They may also notice that the pictures or dolls around the classroom do not look like them, or sense impatience when they need extra time responding in English. All of these examples can be hurtful and negatively affect their self-esteem.

As Dr. Adair points out, "Discrimination can have particularly negative ramifications for the development of young children's sense of self and social identity. If people around children communicate distaste for their appearance, language, or cultural values, children internalize negative views of themselves. Discrimination is particularly harmful in the early years, when children are in the process of developing a sense of self."

"There is evidence that the way children are treated during early schooling affects their later behavior and academic performance. Children who receive negative messages about themselves in school may be less likely to achieve academic success, graduate from school, and ultimately, surpass their parents' economic position."

A form of structural discrimination evident in schools is **low engagement with parents of immigrant children**. Sometimes this is due to communication issues. Either the teacher may feel unable to engage with the immigrant parents or the parents do not feel they can communicate effectively. In certain cases, the teacher may feel the parent who cannot speak English well has nothing to offer the school, and parents may sense discriminatory attitudes by teachers or administrators.

Other times, it is based on different expectations. The teacher may expect the parent to take the lead in approaching the teacher, while in the parents' culture, that may be considered inappropriate. In other instances, the parent cannot get transportation to the school, may not be able to obtain childcare for their younger children, or are unable to take time off from work. "When parents are not connected to schools, they cannot effectively advocate for their children or promote their academic engagement and sense of belonging in school." The struggles to collaborate with immigrant parents are particularly challenging for teachers in geographic areas that had limited diversity in the past.

The MPI report provides guidance for educators to address the problems identified. Below are several recommendations that can be met by utilizing the ideas and lessons presented in this book.

- Consider a balanced approach towards the diverse cultures represented in the classroom. While negative assumptions about immigrant families or cultures are clearly detrimental, it is equally important not to be "colorblind" and assume that all people are the same. Rather, try to get to know the immigrant families and the issues that are important to their cultures. The goal is to accept differences and highlight diversity without judgment.
- Make an extra effort to be patient with immigrant children and parents that do not speak English well. It is extremely beneficial if the teacher can find out more about the cultures represented in the class and learn some words from their students' home languages.
- Welcome parents into the classroom. They are the experts on both their cultures and their children, and they can play important roles in enhancing learning in both the classroom and at home. Teachers can involve an immigrant parent or relative in activities that educate all the children in the classroom while demonstrating the value of diversity. They can also encourage reading in the home language with the use of lending libraries.
- Incorporate the community's diverse cultures and linguistic heritage in instruction. This can be done through lesson plans, games, and crafts. Teachers can also emphasize the value of speaking other languages and maintaining a connection to one's traditions. This encourages children to be proud of their heritage and their families, making them more likely to engage in classroom discussions.
- Encourage students from diverse cultures and with different language skills to work in groups on projects or games. The learning experiences should allow immigrant children to use examples from home and their culture to show their skills and knowledge. By working together, children will experience different ways of thinking and varied approaches to problem solving and communication while learning more about their diverse peers.

This book aims to assist teachers in meeting the above recommendations by giving specific suggestions for incorporating diverse cultures in formal instructional activities and play. It provides ideas for how immigrant parents can enhance learning in the classroom and at home, and includes resources for promoting the use and development of home language learning.

MULTICULTURAL LESSON PLANS

"The highest result of education is tolerance."
- Helen Keller

This section includes eleven multicultural lesson plans that can be used in classrooms or as part of a homeschooling curriculum. The introductory chapter provides an overview of the three main themes of the lesson plans and discusses why we selected these themes and the books highlighted in each lesson. It also reviews research about using dual language books to support children's learning. A bibliography of the cited research works is included at the end of the book. The chapter then outlines the lesson plan structure as well as how the lesson plans are designed to meet several state standards across a range of curricular areas and grade levels.

The following chapters are the multicultural lesson plans, broken down into the three main themes. Each theme has three to four topics (lessons). Each lesson includes detailed information on the objectives, essential questions, required resources, integration across subject areas, vocabulary, procedures, and assessments. The lessons also include ideas for differentiation, extension activities, and flashcards that can be printed for classroom use.

Introduction to Multicultural Lesson Plans

Lesson Plan Themes

In developing this set of lesson plans, we began by exploring some of our favorite dual language books. Our overall aims were twofold: First, we wanted to promote children's cultural awareness, formation of identity, appreciation of diversity, respect for traditions, and tolerance. Second, we aimed to foster positive learning experiences for all children, with a particular focus on dual language learners. With this in mind, we selected ten dual language books that we feel communicate important messages in supporting the development of positive multicultural attitudes for children. The books were categorized into three overarching themes, with each theme guided by a central goal. These overarching themes and corresponding goals are:

1. **Cultural Awareness and Diversity:** To provide children with tools that will allow them to become aware of cultural diversity and to foster relationships based on respect, equality, and diversity.

2. **Folktales, Fables, Myths, and Legends:** To expose students to a range of traditional literature from different cultures and countries, thereby enabling them to appreciate the multitude of stories told to students around the world.

3. **Holidays and Festivals:** To provide children with opportunities to learn about and appreciate a range of holidays and festivals celebrated around the world.

A total of eleven lesson plans are included. One introductory lesson is provided. The purpose of this first lesson is to introduce children to the idea that the identities they have are unique, but that they also share some features of their identities with others. The remaining lesson plans were written using ten dual language books. Each lesson plan uses a new book and builds on ideas introduced in previous lessons. However, we recognize that the facilitator may not have access to all ten dual language books or may not wish to cover every topic pertaining to the lessons. Therefore, the lesson plans were designed in such a way that one book may be selected and taught in isolation.

Theme 1: Cultural Awareness and Diversity

Goal: To provide children with tools that allow them to become aware of cultural diversity and to foster relationships based on respect, equality, and diversity.

"The use of dual language books can support the negotiation of personal identity and highlight aspects of learner identity as children learn to read in their home language."
(Sneddon, 2009, p.43)

The central purpose of this book is to provide an actionable, easy-to-use resource that educators and homeschooling families can use to teach children about other languages and cultures while supporting literacy development and multiculturalism. To this end, we felt that children need to initially develop an awareness and appreciation of cultural diversity and identity, which became our first theme.

Critical components of cultural awareness and diversity concern *identity* and *culture*. In order to develop children's understanding of these concepts, we utilized the following definitions to guide our work.

Thinking about identity, Sneddon (2009) attests that "identities are about how we live our everyday lives...individuals bring with them the traditions and languages of the country of origin and find themselves living with new ones" (p.43). Children in early elementary school grades are undergoing critical periods in the formation of their identities. The use of dual language books offers a prime opportunity for children to learn about their own identity while also moving beyond their egocentrism, to understand and appreciate the identity of others. The facilitator's role is pivotal in supporting this, particularly for dual language learners. Cummins et al. (2005) assert the importance of "creat[ing] environments that affirm the identities of English language learners" (p.39). When children feel that their identities are acknowledged and valued, it increases their motivation to engage in learning (p.39).

Merriam Webster's dictionary defines culture as "the customary beliefs, social forms, and material traits...shared by people in a place or time." A child's cultural background is shaped by several interconnected factors, including, but not limited to, parental values, country of origin, religious beliefs, and ethnicity. With particular regard to dual language learners, it is important to note that "in addition to language barriers, immigrant children may also experience a cultural mismatch between school and home" (Li, 2003, 2006b in Li, 2008, p.154). The use of dual language books works to overcome this barrier as children see their home cultures represented in these picture books. Furthermore, the discussions that these books generate with peers create opportunities to share their cultural experiences with one another.

Theme 2: Folktales, Fables, Myths, and Legends

Goal: To expose students to a range of traditional literature from different cultures and countries, thereby enabling them to appreciate the multitude of stories told to students around the world.

"The world is shaped by two things - stories told and the memories they leave behind."
- Vera Nazarian

The stories we tell our children have much to say about where we have come from as a people in a specific time and place. Of course, no two people will tell a story in the same way, and so no two versions of these stories will be exactly the same. The differences in the versions of these tales highlight the priorities and concerns of the culture from which they are told. However, the central themes or concepts that they are trying to draw attention to are universal. Kindness, honesty, cooperation, friendship, and love, among many other themes, transcend borders and cultures, and are aspects of humanity that we hope all children will experience and exhibit.

Exposing children to a fraction of the wealth of existing folktales, fables, myths, and legends will give them a greater understanding of where the stories they know and love originate. Children will also delight in hearing the tales that are traditional to other countries around the world, drawing commonalities to their own lives and experiences, while at the same time broadening their awareness and appreciation of other cultures.

The stories contained within this theme originate from Russia (*The Giant Turnip*), Ireland (*The Children of Lir*), and China (*Yeh Hsien a Chinese Cinderella*). While some of these stories will be familiar to children, it may be the first time that they hear other stories. We utilized these beloved tales as a platform for discussion about how different cultures tell different stories, using the knowledge gained from this endeavor to further enhance the children's cultural awareness.

15

Theme 3: Holidays and Festivals

Goal: To provide children with opportunities to learn about and appreciate a range of holidays and festivals from around the world.

"Share our similarities, celebrate our differences."
- M. Scott Peck

While the previous theme looked at how culture was passed down from generation to generation, the third theme focuses on how culture is manifested today. Each lesson plan in this section aims to expose children to the diversity of holidays and festivals celebrated around the world. They aim to draw children's attention to similarities and differences between a variety of holidays and festivals, and to encourage children to recognize how holidays and festivals are celebrated differently in other parts of the world. The dual language books selected depict celebrations of four major world holidays and festivals: Chinese New Year (*Li's Chinese New Year*), Ramadan (*Samira's Eid*), Diwali (*Deepak's Diwali*), and Christmas (*Marek and Alice's Christmas*). Background information about each of these holidays and festivals is outlined in the lesson plans and may be used as one source of reference for the facilitator.

Ensuring that there is a representative selection of dual language books that portray a range of cultures and traditions is an important consideration for the facilitator. It is imperative to note that the holidays and festivals depicted in this theme represent a small selection of holidays and festivals celebrated worldwide. Recognizing that many holidays and festivals are not represented in this set of lesson plans, it is suggested that the facilitator provide opportunities for children to discuss similarities and discover differences of other holidays and festivals celebrated by their families. Seeking a balance in this way enables the facilitator to recognize, acknowledge, and value the celebration of other holidays or festivals such as Hanukkah, Wesak, Baisakhi, or Día de los Muertos, which are not depicted in the books.

What the Research Says About Using Dual Language Books to Support Children's Learning

The power of literature is undeniable. For children, picture books can be viewed as windows into another world, enabling the reader to gain exposure to new ideas. However, they may also act as a mirror, allowing us to see ourselves more clearly, understanding our experience through the connections we share, while at the same time increasing our empathy and ability to understand the experiences and feelings of others (Sims Bishop, 1990). Dual language books act as a good entry point and stimulus for promoting cultural awareness and diversity. Using dual language books respects and affirms children's multiple identities (Sneddon, 2009; Cummins et al., 2005), increases student participation and motivation to engage in learning (Sneddon, 2009; Cummins et al., 2005), and celebrates the diversity present in classrooms today (Naqvi, 2009). Given the ever-changing composition of classrooms as mentioned earlier in the book, these are all attitudes and values that are of critical importance in the current educational discourse and practice.

Bilingual books support the learning of dual language learners as well as children who speak English as their first language. Davies Samway and McKeon (2002) note that "there are many parallels between learning a first and second language" (p.62). From a dual language learner's perspective, bilingual books are an underutilized resource for learning English. For the facilitator, dual language books help overcome the challenge of not being familiar with the home language of the child. Furthermore, these books encourage conceptual and meta-linguistic transference between the child's L1 and L2 (Gillanders, Castro, and Franco, 2014; Naqvi et al., 2012; Bialystok, 2004; Roessingh, 2004; Lindholm-Leary, 2000) and are a powerful tool in forging stronger connections between the home and school (Sneddon, 2008; Cummins, 1986, 2000). It is clear from expert discourse in the field that dual language books are an advantageous learning tool from both a cultural and linguistic perspective.

Structure of the Lesson Plans

The lesson plans are designed to be useful in numerous learning environments. Our challenge was to make these lesson plans universal enough so that they can be tailored to suit the individual context in which they are used. Consequently, throughout the lesson plans the term facilitator describes the individual who is working with the children, which may include a teacher, parent, or tutor. Grade levels and allocated time are suggested in the lesson plans. However, these are only a guide and can be adapted to suit the needs and abilities of the students.

Each lesson plan begins by restating the central goal of the theme, the dual language book used, the languages the book is available in, and a snapshot of the lesson. Background information for the facilitator, including sources and helpful links to be used, are also outlined for additional reading. Important vocabulary present in the books is identified and categorized into two main headings: key vocabulary and story-specific vocabulary.

Each lesson plan follows a common structure (listed below) for ease of use:

1. Grade Level
2. Time Frame
3. Objectives
   - Knowledge
   - Skills
   - Attitudes

4. Essential Questions
5. Materials and Resources
6. Linkage and Integration Across Subject Areas
7. Vocabulary to be Developed in Lesson
8. Procedure
    - Introduction
    - Vocabulary Development
    - Reading
    - Discussion (questions)
    - Word Identification/Fluency Development
    - Retell the Story
    - Independent Work/Group Work Activity
    - Conclusion - Revisit Essential Questions
9. Assessment
10. Accommodation/Differentiation
11. Extension Activities
12. Vocabulary Flashcards

The methodologies and strategies proposed cater to differential learning styles and aim to engage children via multiple means of representation, engagement, and expression. Cross-curricular links and extension activities are also included in the lesson plans, taking into account the "need to explicitly plan to provide dual language learners with opportunities to listen and use words in a variety of contexts and on multiple occasions" (Gillanders, Castro, and Franco, 2014, p.215).

Targeting children's vocabulary development plays a key role in strengthening children's comprehension (Bear et al., 2016; Ganske, 2000; Nagy, 2005). Cross-curricular integration reinforces this process of vocabulary development:

"Storybook reading occupies only a small part of the school day, so enhancing other learning opportunities during the classroom routine to promote vocabulary is critical for the development of dual language learners."
(Gillanders et al., 2014, p.219)

The activities suggested span across the curricular areas of language arts, mathematics, science, social studies, music, visual arts, and drama. As with all other areas of the lesson plans, these ideas can be manipulated and adapted to suit the needs of the children. While such activities are complementary to the reading of the dual language book, their focus is ultimately to enrich children's vocabulary development.

Standards

With regard to standards and objectives, these lesson plans are designed to meet several Common Core State Standards across a range of curricular areas and grade levels. Links to the Standards are provided below, allowing the facilitator to select accordingly to their particular context:

1. Common Core State Standards for English Language Arts & Literacy in History/Social Studies, Science, and Technical Subjects: http://www.corestandards.org/wp-content/uploads/ELA_Standards1.pdf
2. Common Core State Standards for Mathematics: http://www.corestandards.org/wp-content/uploads/Math_Standards1.pdf
3. National Core Arts Standards: http://nationalartsstandards.org/
4. English Language Development Standards (WIDA): https://www.wida.us/get.aspx?id=540

Standards Applicable to All Lesson Plan

Common Core State Standards for English Language Arts & Literacy in History/Social Studies, Science, and Technical Subjects

Using 2nd and 4th grade levels as example teaching contexts, we have listed specific standards from the Common Core State Standards for English Language Arts & Literacy in History/Social Studies, Science, and Technical Subjects that are met in each lesson plan:

1. Reading - Literature
2. Reading - Foundational Skills
3. Speaking and Listening
4. Language Standards

2nd Grade - Reading: Literature

CCSS.ELA-LITERACY.RL.2.1: Ask and answer such questions as who, what, where, when, why, and how to demonstrate understanding of key details in a text.

CCSS.ELA-LITERACY.RL.2.2: Recount stories, including fables and folktales from diverse cultures, and determine their central message, lesson, or moral.

CCSS.ELA-LITERACY.RL.2.9: Compare and contrast two or more versions of the same story (e.g., Cinderella stories) by different authors or from different cultures.

2nd Grade - Reading: Foundational Skills

CCSS.ELA-LITERACY.RF.2.4: Read with sufficient accuracy and fluency to support comprehension:

- **CCSS.ELA-LITERACY.RF.2.4.A:** Read grade-level text with purpose and understanding.
- **CCSS.ELA-LITERACY.RF.2.4.B:** Read grade-level text orally with accuracy, appropriate rate, and expression on successive readings.
- **CCSS.ELA-LITERACY.RF.2.4.C:** Use context to confirm or self-correct word recognition and understanding, rereading as necessary.

2nd Grade - Speaking & Listening

CCSS.ELA-LITERACY.SL.2.1: Participate in collaborative conversations with diverse partners about grade 2 topics and texts with peers and adults in small and larger groups:

- **CCSS.ELA-LITERACY.SL.2.1.A:** Follow agreed-upon rules for discussions (e.g., gaining the floor in respectful ways, listening to others with care, speaking one at a time about the topics and texts under discussion).
- **CCSS.ELA-LITERACY.SL.2.1.B:** Build on others' talk in conversations by linking their comments to the remarks of others.
- **CCSS.ELA-LITERACY.SL.2.1.C:** Ask for clarification and further explanation as needed about the topics and texts under discussion.

CCSS.ELA-LITERACY.SL.2.2: Recount or describe key ideas or details from a text read aloud or information presented orally or through other media.

CCSS.ELA-LITERACY.SL.2.3: Ask and answer questions about what a speaker says in order to clarify comprehension, gather additional information, or deepen understanding of a topic or issue.

CCSS.ELA-LITERACY.SL.2.5: Create audio recordings of stories or poems; add drawings or other visual displays to stories or recounts of experiences when appropriate to clarify ideas, thoughts, and feelings.

2nd Grade - Language

CCSS.ELA-LITERACY.L.2.1: Demonstrate command of the conventions of standard English grammar and usage when writing or speaking:

- **CCSS.ELA-LITERACY.L.2.1.B:** Form and use frequently occurring irregular plural nouns (e.g., feet, children, teeth, mice, fish).

- **CCSS.ELA-LITERACY.L.2.1.D:** Form and use the past tense of frequently occurring irregular verbs (e.g., sat, hid, told).

CCSS.ELA-LITERACY.L.2.2.A: Demonstrate command of the conventions of standard English capitalization, punctuation, and spelling when writing - Capitalize holidays, product names, and geographic names.

CCSS.ELA-LITERACY.L.2.5: Demonstrate understanding of word relationships and nuances in word meanings:

- **CCSS.ELA-LITERACY.L.2.5.A:** Identify real-life connections between words and their use (e.g., describe foods that are spicy or juicy).
- **CCSS.ELA-LITERACY.L.2.5.B:** Distinguish shades of meaning among closely related verbs (e.g., toss, throw, hurl) and closely related adjectives (e.g., thin, slender, skinny, scrawny).

CCSS.ELA-LITERACY.L.2.6: Use words and phrases acquired through conversations, reading and being read to, and responding to texts, including using adjectives and adverbs to describe (e.g., when other kids are happy that makes me happy).

4th Grade - Reading: Literature

CCSS.ELA-LITERACY.RL.4.1: Refer to details and examples in a text when explaining what the text says explicitly and when drawing inferences from the text.

CCSS.ELA-LITERACY.RL.4.2: Determine a theme of a story, drama, or poem from details in the text; summarize the text.

CCSS.ELA-LITERACY.RL.4.3: Describe in depth a character, setting, or event in a story or drama, drawing on specific details in the text (e.g., a character's thoughts, words, or actions).

CCSS.ELA-LITERACY.RL.4.9: Compare and contrast the treatment of similar themes and topics (e.g., opposition of good and evil) and patterns of events (e.g., the quest) in stories, myths, and traditional literature from different cultures.

4th Grade - Reading: Foundational Skills

CCSS.ELA-LITERACY.RF.4.4: Read with sufficient accuracy and fluency to support comprehension:

- **CCSS.ELA-LITERACY.RF.4.4.A:** Read grade-level text with purpose and understanding.

- **CCSS.ELA-LITERACY.RF.4.4.B:** Read grade-level prose and poetry orally with accuracy, appropriate rate, and expression on successive readings.
- **CCSS.ELA-LITERACY.RF.4.4.C:** Use context to confirm or self-correct word recognition and understanding, rereading as necessary.

4th Grade - Speaking & Listening

CCSS.ELA-LITERACY.SL.4.1: Engage effectively in a range of collaborative discussions (one-on-one, in groups, and teacher led) with diverse partners on grade 4 topics and texts, building on others' ideas and expressing their own clearly:

- **CCSS.ELA-LITERACY.SL.4.1.B:** Follow agreed-upon rules for discussions and carry out assigned roles.
- **CCSS.ELA-LITERACY.SL.4.1.C:** Pose and respond to specific questions to clarify or follow up on information, and make comments that contribute to the discussion and link to the remarks of others.
- **CCSS.ELA-LITERACY.SL.4.1.D:** Review the key ideas expressed and explain their own ideas and understanding in light of the discussion.

CCSS.ELA-LITERACY.SL.4.2: Paraphrase portions of a text read aloud or information presented in diverse media and formats, including visually, quantitatively, and orally.

CCSS.ELA-LITERACY.SL.4.4: Report on a topic or text, tell a story, or recount an experience in an organized manner, using appropriate facts and relevant, descriptive details to support main ideas or themes; speak clearly at an understandable pace.

4th Grade - Language

CCSS.ELA-LITERACY.L.4.2: Demonstrate command of the conventions of standard English capitalization, punctuation, and spelling when writing:

- **CCSS.ELA-LITERACY.L.4.2.A:** Use correct capitalization.
- **CCSS.ELA-LITERACY.L.4.2.B:** Use commas and quotation marks to mark direct speech and quotations from a text.
- **CCSS.ELA-LITERACY.L.4.2.C:** Use a comma before a coordinating conjunction in a compound sentence.
- **CCSS.ELA-LITERACY.L.4.2.D:** Spell grade-appropriate words correctly, consulting references as needed.

CCSS.ELA-LITERACY.L.4.3: Use knowledge of language and its conventions when writing, speaking, reading, or listening:

- **CCSS.ELA-LITERACY.L.4.3.A:** Choose words and phrases to convey ideas precisely.

- **CCSS.ELA-LITERACY.L.4.3.B:** Choose punctuation for effect.

CCSS.ELA-LITERACY.L.4.4.A: Determine or clarify the meaning of unknown and multiple-meaning words and phrases based on grade 4 reading and content, choosing flexibly from a range of strategies - Use context (e.g., definitions, examples, or restatements in text) as a clue to the meaning of a word or phrase.

CCSS.ELA-LITERACY.L.4.6: Acquire and use accurately grade-appropriate general academic and domain-specific words and phrases, including those that signal precise actions, emotions, or states of being (e.g., quizzed, whined, stammered) and that are basic to a particular topic (e.g., wildlife, conservation, and endangered when discussing animal preservation).

Standards Applicable to Specific Lessons:

As the range of reading response activities included in the lesson plans span the curricular areas of English language arts, mathematics, science, social studies, music, visual arts, and drama, many of these extension activities meet the Writing Standards of the Common Core State Standards for English Language Arts, Common Core State Standards for Mathematics, and The National Core Arts Standards. With this in mind, a selection of extension activities and corresponding standards are provided below:

1. **English Language Arts Writing Activities: Common Core State Standards for English Language Arts & Literacy in History/Social Studies, Science, and Technical Subjects (Writing Standards)**

   - *2nd Grade - Independent Writing Activities (Multiple Lessons):*

     CCSS.ELA-LITERACY.W.2.3: Write narratives in which they recount a well elaborated event or short sequence of events, include details to describe actions, thoughts, and feelings, use temporal words to signal event order, and provide a sense of closure.

     CCSS.ELA-LITERACY.W.2.8: Recall information from experiences or gather information from provided sources to answer a question.

   - *4th Grade - Independent Writing Activities (Multiple Lessons):*

     CCSS.ELA-LITERACY.W.4.4: Produce clear and coherent writing in which the development and organization are appropriate to task, purpose, and audience.

CCSS.ELA-LITERACY.W.4.5: With guidance and support from peers and adults, develop and strengthen writing as needed by planning, revising, and editing. (Editing for conventions should demonstrate command of Language standards 1–3 up to and including grade 4.)

- ***4th Grade - Social Studies Project Work (The Children of Lir; Li's Chinese New Year; Samira's Eid; Deepak's Diwali; Alice and Marek's Christmas):***

  CCSS.ELA-LITERACY.W.4.7: Conduct short research projects that build knowledge through investigation of different aspects of a topic.

- ***4th Grade - Character Sketch (The Children of Lir):***

  CCSS.ELA-LITERACY.W.4.9a: Draw evidence from literary or informational texts to support analysis, reflection, and research - Apply grade 4 Reading standards to literature (e.g., "Describe in depth a character, setting, or event in a story or drama, drawing on specific details in the text [e.g., a character's thoughts, words, or actions].").

2. Mathematics Activities: Common Core State Standards for Mathematics

- ***1st Grade Operations and Algebraic Thinking - The Story of the Number 12 (Li's Chinese New Year):***

  CCSS.MATH.CONTENT.1.OA.C.6: Add and subtract within 20, demonstrating fluency for addition and subtraction within 10. Use strategies such as counting on; making ten (e.g., 8 + 6 = 8 + 2 + 4 = 10 + 4 = 14); decomposing a number leading to a ten (e.g., 13 – 4 = 13 – 3 – 1 = 10 – 1 = 9); using the relationship between addition and subtraction (e.g., knowing that 8 + 4 = 12, one knows 12 – 8 = 4); and creating equivalent but easier or known sums (e.g., adding 6 + 7 by creating the known equivalent 6 + 6 + 1 = 12 + 1 = 13).

- ***2nd Grade Geometry - Tessellation Art (Samira's Eid):***

  CCSS.MATH.CONTENT.2.G.A.3: Partition circles and rectangles into two, three, or four equal shares, describe the shares using the words halves, thirds, half of, a third of, etc., and describe the whole as two halves, three thirds, four fourths. Recognize that equal shares of identical wholes need not have the same shape.

- ***4th Grade Geometry - Rangoli Pattern Symmetry (Deepak's Diwali):***

  CCSS.MATH.CONTENT.4.G.A.3: Recognize a line of symmetry for a two-dimensional figure as a line across the figure such that the figure can be folded along the line into matching parts. Identify line-symmetric figures and draw lines of symmetry.

3. **Dance, Theater, Music, and Visual Arts Activities: National Core Arts Standards**

- ***2nd Grade Dance - Dragon Dance (Li's Chinese New Year):***

  DA:Cr1.1.2a: Explore movement inspired by a variety of stimuli (for example, music/sound, text, objects, images, symbols, observed dance, experiences) and suggest additional sources for movement ideas.

  DA:Pr6.1.2a: Dance for and with others in a space where audience and performers occupy different areas.

  DA:Re7.1.2b: Demonstrate and describe movements in dances from different genres or cultures.

  DA:Re9.1.2a: Observe or demonstrate dances from a genre or culture. Discuss movements and other aspects of the dances that make the dances work well, and explain why they work. Use simple dance terminology.

  DA:Cn11.1.2a: Observe a dance and relate the movement to the people or environment in which the dance was created and performed.

- ***2nd Grade Theater - Drama Response to Text (Multiple Lessons):***

  TH:Cr1.1.2b: Collaborate with peers to conceptualize scenery in a guided drama experience (e.g., process drama, story drama, creative drama).

  TH:Cr3.1.2b: Use and adapt sounds and movements in a guided drama experience (e.g., process drama, story drama, creative drama).

  TH:Pr4.1.2a: Interpret story elements in a guided drama experience (e.g., process drama, story drama, creative drama).

  TH:Pr6.1.2a: Contribute to group guided drama experiences (e.g., process drama, story drama, creative drama) and informally share with peers.

  TH:Re9.1.2a: Collaborate on a scene in a guided drama experience (e.g., process drama, story drama, creative drama).

TH:Re9.1.2b: Use a prop or costume in a guided drama experience (e.g., process drama, story drama, creative drama) to describe characters, settings, or events.

TH:Cn11.2.2a: Identify similarities and differences in stories from multiple cultures in a guided drama experience (e.g., process drama, story drama, creative drama).

- *2nd Grade Music - Listening & Responding to Children of Lir Overture (The Children of Lir):*

MU:Pr4.3.2a: Demonstrate understanding of expressive qualities (such as dynamics and tempo) and how creators use them to convey expressive intent .

- *2nd Grade Music - Singing Lullabies (Welcome to the World Baby):*

MU:Pr6.1.2a: Perform music for a specific purpose with expression and technical accuracy.

MU:Pr6.1.2b: Perform appropriately for the audience and purpose.

- *2nd Grade Music - Listening & Responding to 'Cicha Noc' (Alice and Marek's Christmas):*

MU:Cn11.0.2a: Demonstrate understanding of relationships between music and the other arts, other disciplines, varied contexts, and daily life.

- *2nd Grade Visual Art - Artwork and Craft Activities (Multiple Lessons):*

VA:Cr1.2.2a: Make art or design with various materials and tools to explore personal interests, questions, and curiosity.

VA:Pr51.2a: Distinguish between different materials or artistic techniques for preparing artwork for presentation.

VA:Cn10.1.2a: Create works of art about events in home, school, or community life.

VA:Cn11.1.2a: Compare and contrast cultural uses of artwork from different times and places.

Theme 1:
Cultural Awareness and Diversity

Topic A:
Introduction to the Unit - Names and Identity

Goal: Provide children with tools that will allow them to become aware of cultural diversity and to foster relationships based on respect, equality, and diversity.

Snapshot of Lesson:

- **Games** are used ("Greetings your Majesty" & "Walk the Line if...") to introduce the concept of diversity to the children.

- Children will **discuss** what features of their identity they have in common with their peers, what they have that is specific to their identity, what features of their identity are visible to others, and what features of their identity are invisible to others.

- **Pictures** will be used to encourage the realization of different cultural identities from around the world.

- (Optional): Children will **create a portfolio** of their work in an 'All About Me' folder to be added to and developed throughout this unit.

Background Information for Facilitator

An effective starting point in teaching children about cultural awareness and diversity is to begin with the children's own identities. Each child has a name and that name is linked to their identity. Children's egocentricity at younger ages sometimes makes it difficult for them to be aware of other people and cultures. We need children to realize that each person has their own identity. While they may have parts of their identity that are common to others, there are other parts that are distinct and unique.

It would be helpful to know the background and home lives of the children before beginning this unit on cultural awareness and diversity. This will aid the facilitator in selecting appropriate resources relevant to the cultures and languages represented in the group, particularly when using the dual-language books.

Some of the books that may be helpful as a reference for this lesson include: *Lima's Red Hot Chilli* (by David Mills and Derek Brazell), *Handa's Surprise* (by Eileen Browne), and *Augustus and his Smile* (by Catherine Rayner). These titles are all available through the Language Lizard website: https://www.languagelizard.com/

Informing parents/guardians about this unit on cultural awareness and diversity will aid the facilitator in planning and implementing the lesson plans. A sample note that can be sent to parents/guardians can be found below:

Dear Parent/Guardian,
Over the coming days, we will be working on a unit about cultural awareness and diversity. This unit will explore the cultures and customs of different people from around the world. Children will be using picture books and a variety of activities during this unit. They will also be completing an "All About Me" folder that will allow them to discover and share their own cultural background with the group. If you have any information or materials that you think would be helpful for your child or for the group, I would be very grateful if you could let me know. If you have any questions, concerns, or queries related to this unit, please don't hesitate to contact me.

Yours Sincerely,

_____

For further information, the following websites may be helpful:

- The Pennsylvania State University. (2001). *An overview of diversity awareness.* Retrieved from http://www.wiu.edu/advising/docs/Diversity_Awareness.pdf
- Morris, R.C. & Mims, N.G. (1999). Making classrooms culturally sensitive. *Education and Culture, 16*(1), pp.29-32.
- Southern Poverty Law Centre. (2018). Retrieved from https://www.tolerance.org/

Lesson Plan: Names and Identity

Grade Level: K-3 (Note: The activities in this lesson plan can be tailored to suit the needs of the specific group that is being taught, at the discretion of the facilitator.)

Time Frame: 2/3 30-40 minute sessions.

Objectives:

Knowledge:

- Investigate the origins of their own name and the names of the people in their group.
- Establish an understanding of who they are and what distinguishes them from those around them through the creation of an "All About Me" folder.

Skills:

- Compare, contrast, and explore how differences can be used to create positive relationships and connections between themselves and others.

Attitudes:

- Appreciate that our name is linked to our identity.
- Identify the value of respect for others.

Essential Questions:

- What does diversity mean to me?
- How can we celebrate the diversity of our group and the wider community?
- How can we show respect for the unique qualities of others?

Materials and Resources:

- Poster paper.
- Colored pencils or crayons.
- Photographs of children from a variety of cultures, or alternatively, photographs of the children in the group (from home with parental/guardian permission). (e.g., https://www.boredpanda.com/happy-children-playing/)
- Folders.
- Parents note explaining the home task.

Linkage and Integration Across Subject Areas:

Language Arts: Vocabulary: Self, Community, Respect, Responsibility, Diversity, Oral language development.

Art: "All About Me" folders.

Geography: Locating our group's cultural diversity/families' nationalities on a map of the world.

Vocabulary to be Developed in Lesson:

- identity
- culture
- awareness
- individual
- unique

Procedure:

1. Begin lesson by playing the game "Greetings your majesty" (note: the children should already know their group and the names of the children in their group to play this game).
   - Invite the children to make a circle with their chairs and place one chair outside the circle facing the wall. This is the "throne".
   - Choose a child to go and sit on the "throne" which faces away from the circle of children.
   - Let the child put on a crown and be the Queen/King.
   - Choose another child to approach the Queen/King from behind, indicating that it is that child's turn by pointing to him/her (making sure no one gives away who it is).
   - Invite the child that was selected to creep up behind the Queen/King and to say "Greetings Your Majesty" in a silly voice while the person on the 'throne' has to guess who it may have been.
   - If the child can guess who it may have been from the voice, he/she gets a round of applause and a chorus of "Congratulations Your Majesty" from the rest of the group and the child who crept up gets a turn. The child can have up to 3 guesses.

2. After the game, engage the children in a discussion about how the Queen or King knew who the person was just by the sound of their voice. Get the children to think what the game would be like if they didn't know the people in the room (*would it be harder or easier? Why?*). Try to elicit from the children that we know one another by name and recognize each other, which is why the game works.

3. Follow this activity by asking the children about their names:
   - *What is your first name/second name/surname/full name?*
   - *Do you have a middle name?*
   - *Who chose your name? How did they choose it?*
   - *Does your name mean anything within your family or culturally, do you know?*
   - *Is there anyone in your family with the same name as you? Why is that?*

4. If there are children from different cultures present in the room, this would be a nice opportunity to invite them to tell the group a little about their names to ease the group into identifying different cultures.

5. Show photographs of different children to the group. These photographs should be printed large enough for the whole group to be able to see or pass around. Invite children's responses to the questions:
   - *What part of the world do you think this child lives in? Why do you think that?*
   - *What are they doing in the photograph?*
   - *Do you do this at home?*
   - *Can you find anything in the photograph that is the same/different to you and where you live?*

6. Tell the children who the children in the photographs are. Allow the children to say their names aloud.

7. Introduce children to the word "identity" by asking the children to define it, put it in a sentence, etc. This definition can be used as a working definition for the group for the entire unit. It may be useful to write this definition down and display it somewhere in the room for children to refer to regularly.

8. Explain to the children that we will be creating an "All About Me" folder that explores each person's identity in the group. Each child will be able to write, draw, or stick in pictures that would tell a visitor to the room who they are and what they like to do. Emphasize that their parents/guardians can help at home when the children bring the folders home. The parents should discuss the folders with the children and help them to insert photographs, write a little about themselves, and/or draw pictures (a parental/guardian note home may be required). Encourage children to focus on specific details for this task such as their family origins and family tree.

9. Send the folders home with the children this evening. Encourage them to insert details that they may not even know about themselves yet, with parental/guardian assistance. A helpful question such as: *What parts of your identity can you see/ not see on the outside?* This may get children thinking about the visible and invisible aspects of our cultural makeup.

10. In the next session, follow up on the work of the previous lesson by inviting children to share with one another their work. Circulate around the room as the children are sharing with their pairs/groups and support children through questioning to get them thinking about how their folders compare to those of their peers.

11. Play a game with the children to highlight the things that are common to everyone in the group, distinct to some children in the group, and unique about each person in the group (e.g., Guess who? Walk the line if...).

    Instructions for "Walk the line if...":
    • Ask everyone to gather on one side of the room/line and face towards its center.
    • Identify ground rules:
        i.   No talking, laughing, nonverbal messages during the activity.
        ii. Respect each person by keeping anything that is shared confidential.
    • Call out specific categories/labels/descriptions, and ask that all of those to whom this applies walk to the other side of the room/line (e.g., *walk the line if you wear glasses*).
    • Once there, the child turns and faces the crowd he/she just left.
    • After a few seconds, continue with a new question. Remember, there is no pressure to cross the room/line if they don't feel comfortable doing so.
    • Begin with visible features of the children's identities but then try to get children to think about the hidden features that make up the children's identities also (e.g., *walk the line if you speak a language other than English*).
    • At the conclusion of the activity, discuss what was felt and what was learned.

12. After the activity, invite the children to return to their desks. Engage in discussion about the activity they have just completed:
    • *What parts of our identity do we share in this group? Why do we have these things in common?*
    • *What parts of our identity are different? Why are they different?*
    • *If someone is different than someone else, what does that mean?*
    • *Can you be friends with someone who is different?*

Assessment:

"All About Me" Folder: children create and maintain a folder containing key information about themselves (including written, pictorial, and photographical information). If the folder is used in a school situation, it may be brought between home and school as the unit progresses and may be filled in with parental/guardian assistance. The folders will be used to stimulate discussion with other children and compare and contrast their folders with the folders of other children.

Facilitator Observation: of responses to questioning, of folders.

Facilitator Questioning: from a range of lower to higher order questions.

Accommodations/Differentiation:

Differential Process:

Invite children who may struggle with writing to include more visual elements in their "All About Me" folder, support their responses to questions by modelling the process with advanced children first, pre-teach them important vocabulary around the topic, etc.

Differential Product/Response:

Advanced children can be invited to present their folders to other groups, write extensively about themselves using descriptive language, etc.

Extension Activities:

Inventing new names for themselves – Why would you pick that name?
Creating a family tree of names.
Music – Singing "It's a Small World."
Group jigsaw art project – How do we all fit together?

Theme 1:
Cultural Awareness and Diversity

Topic B:
Culture and Identity –
Welcome to the World Baby

Goal: Provide children with tools that will allow them to become aware of cultural diversity and to foster relationships based on respect, equality, and diversity.

Book Used in Lesson: *Welcome to the World Baby*
Written by Na'ima bint Robert. Illustrated by Derek Brazell.
Available In English with: Albanian, Arabic, Bengali, Bulgarian, Chinese, Croatian, Farsi, French, German, Gujarati, Hindi, Italian, Japanese, Korean, Kurdish, Panjabi, Polish, Portuguese, Romanian, Russian, Shona, Somali, Spanish, Swahili, Turkish, Urdu, Vietnamese, and Yoruba.

Snapshot of Lesson:

- (Optional): **Revisit some of the concepts** of identity and diversity already addressed in the previous lesson using the "All About Me" folders as a stimulus for discussion.

- Children **explore key vocabulary** from the story *Welcome to the World Baby*, **predict** what the story will be about, and **make connections** with the story.

- Children **read** the story of *Welcome to the World Baby* with the facilitator.

- Engage in **discussion** about the story with the children.

- **Retell** the story in their own words.

- (Optional): Children further develop their **"All About Me" folders**, including written or visual elements.

Background Information for Facilitator

The facilitator should be aware of the families and backgrounds of their children. It would be nice to coordinate this lesson with the arrival of a new baby in a child's family, if possible.

The facilitator may pre-teach the children the new vocabulary in the story first so that the children are able to focus on the reading and content of the book during this lesson.

Lesson Plan: *Welcome to the World Baby*

Grade Level: K-3 (Note: The activities in this lesson plan can be tailored to suit the needs of the specific group that is being taught, at the discretion of the facilitator.)

Time Frame: 30-40 minute session.

Objectives:

Knowledge:

- Review the concepts of identity and diversity.

- Apply the knowledge gained from these concepts by looking at their own lives and how their identity has emerged since birth.

Skills:

- Identify, define, and use the new vocabulary in the story.
- Enhance their comprehension strategies using literal, inferential, and evaluative questioning.
- Practice their summarization skills using the story as an anchor text.
- Explore the alternative languages of the text for similarities and differences.

Attitudes:

- Understand and appreciate how a baby's identity is shaped (from his/her family) using literature: *Welcome to the World Baby.*

Essential Questions:

- How do the different children welcome a new baby into their families?
- How do different families welcome babies into the world?

Materials and Resources:

- "All About Me" folders.
- *Welcome to the World Baby* by Na'ima bint Robert & Derek Brazell.
- New vocabulary flashcards and pictures.
- Talking object (e.g., ball) to signify whose turn it is to talk during discussion.
- PENpal Audio Recorder Pen (optional).

Linkage and Integration Across Subject Areas:

Language Arts/Reading: Engaging with literature.

Art: Creation of the "All About Me" folders.

Geography: Locating where in the world the baby welcoming traditions originate.

Vocabulary to be Developed in Lesson:

Key Vocabulary		Story Specific Vocabulary
• welcome • senses • good luck • birth • life • growth • whispered • cheered	• celebration • coins • shining • eagerly • delicious	• stroking • envelope • lock of hair • ribbon • jewelers • fortune • aloe leaf • newborn

Procedure:

Introduction:

1. Review the content covered in the previous lessons by asking some of the children to share any new items they have added to their "All About Me" folders. If this is the first lesson in the unit being taught, it is possible to skip this step.

2. Show children the cover of the book *Welcome to the World Baby*. Ask their predictions about the book using guided questions:
    *   *What does the word "welcome" mean? What sorts of things might you welcome?*
    *   *When might you use the word welcome?*
    *   *Who is welcoming the baby? Why are they doing that?*
    *   *How do you think the children on the cover feel about welcoming the baby? Why are they feeling this way?*

3. Invite the children to talk about babies before reading the book:
    *   *Do you have a baby brother/sister?*
    *   *Do you remember when he/she joined your family? Did you do anything special? What did you do?*
    *   *Did your family do anything special to welcome you to the family when you were a baby?*

Vocabulary Development:

4. Engage in vocabulary development with the children using the list of words above or any additional words as is deemed appropriate. Using flashcards, pictures, or interactive whiteboard slides, invite the children to identify, say, use, count syllables, and define the new terms in their own words. You may wish to pre-teach the vocabulary first.

Reading:

5. Elicit children's predictions about the book or any connections they may have based on the book's title and cover. Connections may be *text-to-text* (what does the child notice from one book/story to another book/story), *text-to-self* (what does the child notice from the book in relation to his/her own lived experiences), or *text-to-wider-world* (what does the child notice from the book in relation to real world historical or current contexts). Read the blurb at the back of the book to help shape their predictions.

6. Read the book with the children, ideally sitting together so you can show them the pictures while reading. This can be done by conducting a read-aloud, getting the children to read sections after the facilitator (echo reading), all reading it together (choral reading), or reading a sentence each between facilitator and child (see-saw reading). Read with appropriate tone, pace, inflection, and enthusiasm to engage the children as much as possible. If there are children who speak the language of the dual language book, here would be a nice opportunity to get them to read/translate a section if they would like, or to identify some words they can recognize in the print. In addition, if the PENpal Audio Recorder Pen is available, the children could hear the book read in English or another language.

Discussion to Encourage Reflection and Response:

7. Invite the children to share anything they enjoyed, connected with, didn't understand, or wanted to question through the use of a talking object. This can be passed around the circle and only the child who has the talking object may speak, encouraging careful listening and turn-taking skills.

8. Ask a range of literal, inferential, and evaluative questions to gauge comprehension of the text (selected at the discretion of the facilitator):

Literal Questions:

(Readers use information taken directly from the text to answer this type of question.)

   i.   *What day of the week did Tariq see his new baby brother in his mum's bed?*
   ii. *What was the teacher's name?*
   iii. *What color was the egg that An-Mei brought in?*

Inferential Questions:

(Reader must use the information in the text to deduce the answer to this type of question.)

   i.   *Why do you think that they wanted to teach the baby that some things can be bitter and some things can be sweet in life?*

39

ii. *In what ways did the students in the class use all their senses?*

Evaluative Questions:

(Reader uses their own knowledge to explore answers to this type of question.)

i. *How do you think the students were feeling as they could see Tariq's mum getting bigger and bigger? Why do you think they felt this way?*
ii. *Which of the customs/traditions of welcoming a new baby did you like best? Why?*
iii. *Looking at the picture of the Five Senses Party, would you say everyone is enjoying themselves? How do you know? What are they doing?*

Word identification/Fluency Development:

9. **Summarizing the Story:** Break the children into pairs. Challenge the children to see if they can take turns at summarizing the story in one breath. This may take some modeling at a whole-group level a few times first in order for the children to grasp the idea. Support the children to help them realize that they must include the main characters, plot, ending, etc.

10. **Revisit the Story and Identify Key Vocabulary Words:** Allow children to revisit some of the vocabulary of the story using the flashcards. For example, the students could reread a section of the story and raise their hands as soon as they hear or see a new vocabulary word, or play language/word games (e.g., charades, hangman/snowman).

Independent Work/Group Work Activity:

11. **"All About Me" folder work:** Explain to the children that they will be adding to their "All About Me" folders in the coming days. They can include pictures of themselves as babies, pictures of family members as babies, write/draw about how new babies are welcomed into their families, etc.

Conclusion:

12. At this point, the facilitator may want to revisit the essential questions to determine whether the children have understood the main ideas of the lesson:
    • *How do the different students welcome a new baby into their families?*
    • *How do different families welcome babies into the world?*

    As a concluding consolidation activity, invite the children to discuss these questions with the whole group, in smaller groups, in pairs, or as a written reflection.

Assessment:

"All About Me" Folder: children can add to the folder, including baby pictures of themselves or other family members.

Facilitator Observation: of responses to questioning, of folders.

Facilitator Questioning: from a range of lower to higher order questions.

Accommodations/Differentiation:

Differential Product/Response:

- Ask higher-order thinking questions of the advanced students.
- Encourage advanced children to contribute more written elements to their "All About Me" folders.

Differential Processes:

- Provide extra wait time and language scaffolds/supports for students who need them (e.g., showing pages from the book, sentence starters).
- All students (but especially English language learners, or ELLs) will benefit from pictures accompanying the vocabulary to be learned in the story.
- For ELLs, it may be helpful to allow the child to take home the dual language book either before or after the lesson. It can then be read at home in the home language before class engagement to promote students' confidence in talking about the book in class. If possible, ask the parents to record the book being read in the home language. The book and recording can then be brought into school so that other students can see and hear some of the home languages spoken by their classmates, deepening their appreciation for language diversity.

Extension Activities:

- **Geography:** Explore additional customs and traditions to welcome babies around the world
- **Music:** Learn some lullabies from around the world and sing them together (e.g., Rockabye Baby https://www.youtube.com/watch?v=6euXT0ruxno, Hush Little Baby https://www.youtube.com/watch?v=JXDTKKwaWh4, Too Ra Loo Ra https://www.youtube.com/watch?v=huHcVxEzABU)

Vocabulary Flashcards for *Welcome to the World Baby:*

welcome	celebration	stroking
senses	coins	envelope
good luck	shining	lock of hair
birth	eagerly	ribbon
life	delicious	jewelers
growth	newborn	fortune
whispered	cheered	aloe leaf

Theme 1:
Cultural Awareness and Diversity

Topic C:
Culture and Identity –
The Wibbly Wobbly Tooth

Goal: Provide children with tools that will allow them to become aware of cultural diversity and to foster relationships based on respect, equality, and diversity.

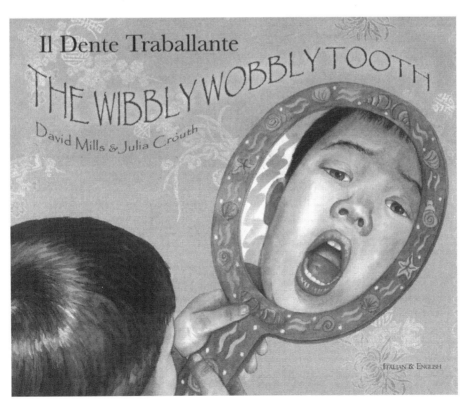

Book Used in Lesson: *The Wibbly Wobbly Tooth*
Written by David Mills. Illustrated by Julia Crouth.
Available In English with: Albanian, Arabic, Bengali, Chinese, Farsi, French, German, Hindi, Italian, Japanese, Korean, Polish, Spanish, Urdu, and Vietnamese.

Snapshot of Lesson:

- (Optional): **Revisit some of the concepts** of identity and diversity already addressed in the previous lesson using the "All About Me" folders as a stimulus for discussion.

- Children **explore key vocabulary** from the story *Welcome to the World Baby*, **predict** what the story will be about, and **make connections** with the story.

- Children **read** the story of *Welcome to the World Baby* with the facilitator.

- Engage in **discussion** about the story with the children.

- **Retell** the story in their own words.

- (Optional): Children further develop their **"All About Me" folders**, including written or visual elements.

- Investigate parts of the mouth/teeth using a mirror/partner work

Background Information for Facilitator

The facilitator should be aware of the families and backgrounds of their children. It would be nice to coordinate this lesson with the loss of a tooth in the room.

The facilitator may pre-teach the children the new vocabulary in the story first so that the children are able to focus on the reading and content of the book during this lesson.

Dental Health Information/Resources/Interactives:
- Colgate-Palmolive Company. (2018). *Brushing and flossing.* Retrieved from: http://www.colgate.com/en/us/oc/oral-health/basics/brushing-and-flossing
- The Nemours Foundation. (2018). *Taking care of your teeth.* Retrieved from http://kidshealth.org/en/kids/teeth-care.html
- Canadian Pediatric Society. (2018). *Healthy teeth for children.* Retrieved from https://www.caringforkids.cps.ca/handouts/healthy_teeth_for_students
- American Dental Association. (2018). *Games and quizzes.* Retrieved from http://www.mouthhealthykids.org/en/games-and-quizzes

Losing teeth traditions around the world:

- Delta Dental. (2016). *Baby tooth traditions around the world.* Retrieved from http://www.cdschools.org/cms/lib04/PA09000075/Centricity/Domain/20/Baby%20tooth%20poster.pdf
- Oral Answers. (2011). *tooth traditions from around the world: It's not just the tooth fairy!* Retrieved from https://www.oralanswers.com/tooth-traditions-world/

Lesson Plan: *The Wibbly Wobbly Tooth*

Grade Level: K-3 (Note: The activities in this lesson plan can be tailored to suit the needs of the specific group that is being taught, at the discretion of the facilitator.)

Time Frame: 30-40 minute session.

Objectives:

Knowledge:

- Review the concepts of identity and diversity.
- Apply the knowledge gained from these concepts by looking at their own lives and how their identity is formed by family and community experiences.
- Learn about the different parts of the mouth and functions of teeth.

Skills:

- Identify, define, and use the new vocabulary in the story.
- Enhance their comprehension strategies using literal, inferential, and evaluative questioning.
- Practice their summarization skills using the story as an anchor text.
- Explore the alternative languages of the text for similarities and differences.
- Draw or shade in a diagram to indicate the teeth that they have lost.

Attitudes:

- Understand and appreciate how our culturally-influenced identity may differ from others.
- Respect that cultural diversity is a present and necessary aspect of life using the room as a microcosm of society.

Essential Questions:

- What do the different children do when they lose a tooth?
- How do different family cultures affect what children do with a lost tooth?

Materials and Resources:

- "All About Me" folders.
- *The Wibbly Wobbly Tooth* by David Mills & Julia Crouth.
- New vocabulary flashcards and pictures.
- Talking object (e.g., ball) to signify whose turn it is to talk during discussion.
- Mirror.
- Teeth diagram/worksheet.
- PENpal Audio Recorder Pen (optional).

Linkage and Integration Across Subject Areas:

Language Arts/Reading: Engaging with literature.

Art: Creation of the "All About Me" folders.

Science: Looking at teeth in the mirror and examining peers' mouths to see teeth lost.

Vocabulary to be Developed in Lesson:

Key Vocabulary		Story Specific Vocabulary
• tooth • burshing • lunch • missed • wanted • pillow • throw • river • roof • nothing • happened • minutes • beautiful	• extremely • careful • wiggled • twisted • tongue • rushed • whispered • wish • neighbor (neighbour) • might • chew	• Li • wibble • wobble • tooth fairy

Procedure:

Introduction:

1. Review the content covered in the previous lessons by asking some of the children to share any new items they have added to their "All About Me" folders.

2. Initiate discussion about teeth and the mouth by getting children to show where their lips, teeth, tongue, and cheeks are. Here children can be supported in using correct language and new language can be introduced (e.g., taste, taste buds, flavor).

3. Show children the cover of the book *The Wibbly Wobbly Tooth*. Ask their predictions about the book using guiding questions:
   - *What do you think the story will be about? Why do you think this?*
   - *What is the boy doing on the cover? Why is he doing this?*
   - *What sorts of things wibble and wobble?*

4. Invite the children to talk about losing teeth before reading the book:
   - *What types of teeth are there? (baby teeth and adult teeth)*
   - *Why do you think they are called baby teeth?*
   - *Why do they fall out?*
   - *Have you or any family members lost a tooth? What was it like?*
   - *What did you do with the tooth?*
   - *How many teeth have you lost?*
   - *How many teeth do you have?*

Vocabulary Development:

5. Engage in vocabulary development with the children using the list of words above or any additional words as is deemed appropriate. Using flashcards, pictures, or interactive whiteboard slides, invite the children to identify, say, use, count syllables, and define the new terms in their own words. It may be advisable to pre-teach the vocabulary first.

Reading:

6. Ask for children's predictions about the book or any connections they may have based on the book's title and cover. Connections may be *text-to-text* (what does the child notice from one book/story to another book/story), *text-to-self* (what does the child notice from the book in relation to his/her own lived experiences), or *text-to-wider-world* (what does the child notice from the book in relation to real world historical or current contexts). Read the blurb at the back of the book to help shape their predictions.

7. Read the book with the children, ideally sitting together so you can show them the pictures while reading. This can be done by conducting a read-aloud, getting the children to read sections after the facilitator (echo reading), all reading it together (choral reading), or reading a sentence each between facilitator and child (see-saw reading). Read with appropriate tone, pace, inflection, and enthusiasm to engage the children as much as possible. If there are children who speak the language of the dual language book, here would be a nice opportunity to get them to read/translate a section if they would like, or to identify some words they can recognize in the print. In addition, if the PENpal Audio Recorder Pen is available, the children could hear the book read in English or another language.

Discussion to Encourage Reflection and Response:

8. Invite the children to share anything they enjoyed, connected with, didn't understand, or wanted to question through the use of a talking object. This can be passed around the circle and only the child who has the talking object may speak, encouraging careful listening and turn-taking skills in the children.

9. Ask a range of literal, inferential, and evaluative questions to gauge comprehension of the text (selected at the discretion of the facilitator):

Literal Questions:

(Readers use information taken directly from the text to answer this type of question.)

    i. *What caused Li's tooth to eventually fall out?*
    ii. *Who did Li go to see with his dad when his tooth fell out?*

Inferential Questions:

(Reader must use the information in the text to deduce the answer to this type of question.)

    i. *Why do you think the next day after Li lost his tooth that nothing happened?*
    ii. *What is it about Grandma that made Li's dad say "she'll know what to do"?*

Evaluative Questions:

(Reader uses their own knowledge to explore answers to this type of question.)

    i. *How do you think Li felt before his tooth fell out and while it was wibbling and wobbling?*
    ii. *How do you think Li felt after he lost his tooth? Where in the story can we find a clue about this?*

Word identification/Fluency Development:

10. **Summarizing the story:** Break the children into pairs. Challenge the children to see if they can take turns at summarizing the story in one breath. This may take some modeling at a whole-group level a few times first in order for the children to grasp the idea. Support the children to help them realize that they must include the main characters, plot, ending, etc.

11. **Revisit the story and identify key vocabulary words:** Allow children to revisit some of the vocabulary of the story using the flashcards. For example, the students could reread a section of the story and raise their hands as soon as they hear or see a new vocabulary word, or play language/word games (e.g., charades, hangman/snowman).

Independent Work/Group Work Activity:

12. **"All About Me" folder work:** Explain to the children that they will be adding to their "All About Me" folders in the coming days. They can include pictures and memories of them losing their teeth, as well as information about their family or culture's customs associated with teeth.

13. **Drawing and Observation Exercise:**
    Children can work in pairs or use mirrors to identify what teeth they have lost, which are baby teeth, etc. They can draw a diagram of their mouths and color in/shade which teeth they have lost.

Conclusion:

14. At this point, the facilitator may want to revisit the essential questions to determine whether the children have understood the main ideas of the lesson:
    • *What do the different students do when they lose a tooth?*
    • *How do different family cultures affect what children do with a lost tooth?*

    As a concluding consolidation activity, invite the children to discuss these questions with the whole group, in smaller groups, in pairs, or as a written reflection.

Assessment:

"All About Me" Folder: children can add to the folder, including pictures of themselves or family members when they lost a tooth.

Facilitator Observation: of responses to questioning, of folders.

Facilitator Questioning: from a range of lower to higher order questions.

Teeth Diagram Task: identifying what teeth the children have lost, observation of their own mouths and peers.

Accommodations/Differentiation:

Differential Product/Response:

- Ask higher-order thinking questions of the advanced students.
- Encourage advanced children to contribute more written elements to their "All About Me" folder

Differential Processes:

- Provide extra wait time and language scaffolds/supports for students who need them (e.g., showing pages from the book, sentence starters).
- For children who are able, invite them to complete their own diagrams of their teeth. For children who may struggle with this task, a pre-drawn teeth diagram may be used which they can color in themselves.
- All students (but especially English language learners or ELLs) will benefit from pictures accompanying the vocabulary to be learned in the story.
- For ELLs, it may be helpful to allow the child to take home the dual language book either before or after the lesson. It can then be read at home in the home language before class engagement to promote students' confidence in talking about the book in class. If possible, ask the parents to record the book being read in the home language. The book and recording can then be brought into school so that other students can see and hear some of the home languages spoken by their classmates, deepening their appreciation for language diversity.

Extension Activities:

- **Science:** Teeth, the mouth, and food.
- **Health:** Brushing teeth and oral hygiene, trying new foods, the food pyramid.
- **Geography:** Identifying teeth traditions from around the world
- **Social Studies:** Explore additional customs and traditions for losing teeth.

Vocabulary Flashcards for *The Wibbly Wobbly Tooth:*

tooth	extremely	Li
burshing	careful	wibble
lunch	wiggled	wobble
missed	twisted	tooth fairy
wanted	tongue	roof
pillow	rushed	nothing
throw	whispered	happened
river	wish	minutes
might	neighbor (neighbour)	beautiful
chew		

Theme 1:
Cultural Awareness and Diversity

Topic D:
Culture and Identity –
Mei Ling's Hiccups

Goal: Provide children with tools that will allow them to become aware of cultural diversity and to foster relationships based on respect, equality, and diversity.

Book Used in Lesson: *Mei Ling's Hiccups*
Written by David Mills. Illustrated by Derek Brazell.
Available In English with: Arabic, Chinese, Czech, French, Japanese, Latvian, Polish, and Spanish.

Snapshot of Lesson:

- (Optional): **Revisit some of the concepts** of identity and diversity already addressed in the previous lesson using the "All About Me" folders as a stimulus for discussion.

- Teach and sing **"The Hiccups Song"** with the children.

- Children explore key vocabulary from the story of *Mei Ling's Hiccups*, predict what the story will be about, and make connections with the story.

- Children **read** the story of *Mei Ling's Hiccups*, with the facilitator.

- Engage in **discussion** about the story with the children.

- **Retell** the story in their own words.

- Children develop and invent **their own methods to get rid of hiccups** which they can present using a choice of mediums.

- (Optional): Children further develop their **"All About Me" folders**, including written or visual elements.

Background Information for Facilitator

The facilitator should be aware of the families and backgrounds of their children.

The facilitator may pre-teach the children the new vocabulary in the story first so that the children are able to focus on the reading and content of the book during this lesson.

A nice idea is to teach the children "The Hiccups Song" (Classic MusicMan. (2012). *The Hiccups Song with Lyrics*. Retrieved from https://www.youtube.com/watch?v=P3jqGhA-WAH4) in advance of the lesson so that they will be pre-exposed to some of the vocabulary of the story first.

Some additional sources of information can be found here:
- The Nemours Foundation. (2018). *What causes hiccups?* Retrieved from http://kidshealth.org/en/kids/hiccup.html
- Nordqvist, C. (2017). *How to cure hiccups*. Retrieved from https://www.medicalnewstoday.com/articles/9896.php

- The Fact Site. (2018). 20 *crazy ways to cure hiccups*. Retrieved from https://www.thefactsite.com/2015/11/20-crazy-cures-for-hiccups.html

Lesson Plan: *Mei Ling's Hiccups*

Grade Level: K-3 (Note: The activities in this lesson plan can be tailored to suit the needs of the specific group that is being taught, at the discretion of the facilitator.)

Time Frame: 30-40 minute session.

Objectives:

Knowledge:

- Review the concepts of identity and diversity.
- Apply the knowledge gained from these concepts by looking at their own lives and how their identity has emerged since birth.
- Investigate how hiccups work and explore where the diaphragm muscle is.

Skills:

- Identify, define, and use the new vocabulary in the story.
- Enhance their comprehension strategies using literal, inferential, and evaluative questioning.
- Practice their summarization skills using the story as an anchor text.
- Explore the alternative languages of the text for similarities and differences.
- Compare the methods of getting rid of hiccups from around the world and utilize this knowledge in devising their own method of getting rid of hiccups.

Attitudes:

- Understand and appreciate that cultural differences exist among people in their group.

Essential Questions:

- What are the different cultural customs used to get rid of hiccups?
- Why do you think different people have different customs for getting rid of hiccups?

Materials and Resources:

- "All About Me" folders.
- *Mei Ling's Hiccups* by David Mills & Derek Brazell.
- New vocabulary flashcards and pictures.
- Talking object (e.g., ball) to signify whose turn it is to talk during discussion.
- "The Hiccups Song" YouTube video https://www.youtube.com/watch?v=P3jqGhAWAH4
- PENpal Audio Recorder Pen (optional).

Linkage and Integration Across Subject Areas:

Language Arts/Reading: Engaging with literature.

Art: Creation of the "All About Me" folders.

Geography: Locating where in the world the hiccup traditions originate.

Vocabulary to be Developed in Lesson:

Key Vocabulary		Story Specific Vocabulary
• everyone • bicyles • balloon • slowly • shouted • listened • carefully • quietly	• yummy • giggled • plugged	• party games • Mei Ling • hicc • hiccups

Procedure:

Introduction:

1. Review the content covered in the previous lessons by asking some of the children to share any new items they have added to their 'All About Me' folders.

2. Play "The Hiccups Song" video for the children. Teach the song line by line. Opportunities exist here for exploration with musical instruments, voice, actions, and singing in parts. (https://www.youtube.com/watch?v=P3jqGhAWAH4)

3. Show children the cover of the book *Mei Ling's Hiccups*. Elicit their predictions about the book using guided questions:
   - *What are hiccups?*
   - *How do you get hiccups?*
   - *How do you get rid of hiccups?*
   - *Who do you think has hiccups on the cover of the book? Why do you think that?*
   - *Why do you think this character got hiccups?*
   - *What's going on in the cover picture?*

Vocabulary Development:

4. Engage in vocabulary development with the children using the list of words above or any additional words as is deemed appropriate. Using flashcards, pictures, or interactive whiteboard slides, invite the children to identify, say, use, count syllables, and define the new terms in their own words. It is also advisable to pre-teach the vocabulary first.

Reading:

5. Elicit children's predictions about the book or any connections they may have based on the book's title and cover. Connections may be *text-to-text* (what does the child notice from one book/story to another book/story), *text-to-self* (what does the child notice from the book in relation to his/her own lived experiences), or *text-to-wider-world* (what does the child notice from the book in relation to real world historical or current contexts). Read the blurb at the back of the book to help shape their predictions.

6. Read the book with the children, ideally sitting together so you can show them the pictures while reading. This can be done by conducting a read-aloud, getting the children to read sections after the facilitator (echo reading), all reading it together (choral reading), or reading a sentence each between facilitator and child (see-saw reading). Read with appropriate tone, pace, inflection, and enthusiasm to engage the children as much as possible. If there are children who speak the language of the dual language book, here would be a nice opportunity to get them to read/translate a section if they would like, or to identify some words they can recognize in the print. In addition, if the PENpal Audio Recorder Pen is available, the children could hear the book read in English or another language.

Discussion to Encourage Reflection and Response:

7. Invite the children to share anything they enjoyed, connected with, didn't understand, or wanted to question through the use of a talking object. This can be passed around

the circle and only the child who has the talking object may speak, encouraging careful listening and turn-taking skills in the children.

8. Ask a range of literal, inferential, and evaluative questions to gauge comprehension of the text (selected at the discretion of the facilitator):

Literal Questions:

(Readers use information taken directly from the text to answer this type of question.)

    i. *What was Mei Ling doing before she got the hiccups?*
    ii. *What were some of the ideas that her friends had to get rid of the hiccups? Can you remember all five?*

Inferential Questions:

(Reader must use the information in the text to deduce the answer to this type of question.)

    i. *Why do you think the class was having a party? (Use the pictures to help you.)*
    ii. *How did the students feel once the teacher came back into the classroom after they had popped the balloons?*

Evaluative Questions:

(Reader uses their own knowledge to explore answers to this type of question.)

    i. *What way would you have used to get rid of the hiccups?*
    ii. *Would you have used any of the students' ways in the story? Why? Why not?*
    iii. *Do you think Mei Ling's hiccups were gone before the teacher came back into the room? Why? Why not?*

Word identification/Fluency Development:

9. **Summarizing the Story:** Break the children into pairs. Challenge the children to see if they can take turns at summarizing the story in one breath. This may take some modeling at a whole-group level a few times first in order for the children to grasp the idea. Support the children to help them realize that they must include the main characters, plot, ending, etc.

10. **Revisit the Story and Identify Key Vocabulary Words:** Allow children to revisit some of the vocabulary of the story using the flashcards. For example, the students could

reread a section of the story and raise their hands as soon as they hear or see a new vocabulary word, or play language/word games (e.g., charades, hangman/snowman).

Independent Work/Group Work Activity:

11. ***Exploring How Hiccups Work:***
    Use some of the websites in the "Background Information for the Facilitator" section of the lesson plan to teach the children how hiccups occur and to describe some traditions around the world to get rid of hiccups. Here, it is possible to get children to do some breathing exercises to enable them to feel their diaphragms.

12. ***Imagining a New Cure for Hiccups Activity:***
    Allow the children in pairs or groups to come up with a wacky idea of their own to get rid of hiccups. They can write, draw pictures, dramatize, sing, or write a poem, which can then be presented to the group.

Conclusion:

13. At this point, the facilitator may want to revisit the essential questions to determine whether the children have understood the main ideas of the lesson:
    * *What are the different cultural customs used to get rid of hiccups?*
    * *Why do you think different people have different customs for getting rid of hiccups?*

    As a concluding consolidation activity, invite the children to discuss these questions with the whole group, in smaller groups, in pairs, or as a written reflection.

Assessment:

"All About Me" Folder: children can add relevant information to the folder.

Facilitator Observation: of responses to questioning, of folders.

Facilitator Questioning: from a range of lower to higher order questions.

Variety of Assessment Methods: utilized during group hiccup presentations.

Accommodations/Differentiation:

Differential Product/Response:

* Ask higher-order thinking questions of the advanced students.

- Encourage advanced children to contribute more written elements to their "All About Me" folder and hiccup presentations

Differential Processes:

- Provide extra wait time and language scaffolds/supports for students who need them (e.g., showing pages from the book, sentence starters).
- All students (but especially English language learners, or ELLs) will benefit from pictures accompanying the vocabulary to be learned in the story.
- For ELLs, it may be helpful to allow the child to take home the dual language book either before or after the lesson. It can then be read at home in the home language before class engagement to promote students' confidence in talking about the book in class. If possible, ask the parents to record the book being read in the home language. The book and recording can then be brought into school so that other students can see and hear some of the home languages spoken by their classmates, deepening their appreciation for language diversity.

Extension Activities

- **Science:** Exploring where and how the diaphragm works. Potential to make a lung model with a diaphragm:
  Selectsoft Publishing. (2011). *Kid Science - Balloon Lung*. Retrieved from https://www.youtube.com/watch?v=vRv2zYH5p9k
- **Music:** Vocal warm-ups and exercising the diaphragm muscle using shallow and deep breathing.
- **Social Studies:** Explore additional customs and traditions to get rid of hiccups around the world

Vocabulary Flashcards for *Mei Ling's Hiccups:*

everyone	yummy	party games
bicycles	giggled	Mei Ling
balloon	plugged	hicc
slowly	carefully	hiccups
shouted	quietly	listened

Theme 2:
Folktales, Fables, Myths, and Legends

Topic A:
Folktales –
The Giant Turnip

Goal: Expose students to a range of traditional literature from different cultures and countries, thereby enabling them to appreciate the multitude of stories told to students around the world.

Book Used in Lesson: *The Giant Turnip*
Adapted by Henriette Barkow. Illustrated by Richard Johnson.
Available In English with: Albanian, Arabic, Bengali, Bulgarian, Chinese, Czech, Farsi, French, German, Hungarian, Italian, Lithuanian, Panjabi, Polish, Portuguese, Romanian, Russian, Somali, Spanish, Tamil, Turkish, Urdu, and Yoruba.

Snapshot of Lesson:

- Playing **20 questions** with a mystery item (turnip) to engage and prepare students.

- **Map work** to identify where in the world the story originated (Russia).

- Children **explore key vocabulary** from the story of *The Giant Turnip*, **predict** what the story will be about, and **make connections** with the story.

- Children **read** the story of *The Giant Turnip* with the facilitator.

- Engage in **discussion** about the story with the children.

- **Retell** the story in their own words.

- **Drama activity**: recreating scenes from the story in groups.

- **Exploring food related vocabulary** and differences in terms between U.S. and U.K. English

Background Information for Facilitator

It is important that the facilitator makes students aware of the difference between folktales, fables, myths, and legends. Further information can be found here:

- East of England Broadband Network. (2006). *Teachers' resources: What are myths, legends and folktales?* Retrieved from http://myths.e2bn.org/teacher/adults/info311-what-are-myths-legends-and-folktales.html
- Andie Worsley. (2017). *Traditional Literature: Folktales, Fairytales, and Fables.* Retrieved from https://www.youtube.com/watch?v=eaVh8yGbXNc

The story in this lesson plan was adapted from a Russian folktale. Written by Aleksey Nikolayevich Tolstoy, *The Enormous Turnip* was included in the collection *Russian Folk Tales*, edited and published by Aleksandr Afanas'ev. Potential exists here to read a more original version of the story either before or after this adapted version and encourage children to note the similarities and differences between the versions. Students can be invited to comment on why they think certain changes were made and other elements of the story were kept.

It may be a good idea to pre-teach the students the new vocabulary in the story first so that they are able to focus on the reading and content of the book during this lesson.

Lesson Plan: *The Giant Turnip*

Grade Level: K-3 (Note: The activities in this lesson plan can be tailored to suit the needs of the specific group that is being taught, at the discretion of the facilitator.)

Time Frame: 30-40 minute session.

Objectives:

Knowledge:

- Identify the origins of the story of *The Giant Turnip.*
- List some of the stories the children have heard growing up.

Skills:

- Identify, define, and use the new vocabulary in the story.
- Enhance their comprehension strategies using literal, inferential, and evaluative questioning.
- Practice their summarization skills using the story as an anchor text.
- Explore the alternative languages of the text for similarities and differences.
- Discuss and explain how this adapted version of the story differs from the original version.
- Compare and contrast some of the different language used to describe foods in different cultures.

Attitudes:

- Understand and appreciate that everyone does not have the same cultural tales and traditional stories around the world by using *The Giant Turnip* as an example of a traditional tale from another country.

Essential Questions:

- What is the main message of the story of *The Giant Turnip*?

Materials and Resources:

- *The Giant Turnip* by Henriette Barkow.
- Turnip/Rutabaga.
- Mystery box big enough to hold the turnip inside.
- New vocabulary flashcards and pictures.
- Talking object (e.g., ball) to signify whose turn it is to talk during discussion.
- PENpal Audio Recorder Pen (optional).

Linkage and Integration Across Subject Areas:

Language Arts/Reading: Engaging with literature.

Drama: Recreating the scene from the story.

Geography: Locating where in the world the story originates.

Vocabulary to be Developed in Lesson:

Key Vocabulary		Story Specific Vocabulary
• fruit • vegetables • spring • prepared • digging • raking • frost • planted • rope • grabbed • strength • stronger	• weeds • recovered • suggested • enormous • joy	• lettuce • radish • carrot • tomato • sunflower • pea • turnip • bulldozer • wobbled • feast • helicopter

Procedure:

Introduction:

1. Show students your mystery box and tell them that there is a very important item inside that they are going to have to identify.

2. Play a game of 20 questions with the students to guess what is in the mystery box. Model and scaffold the students to ask broad, categorical questions such as: *Is it a living thing? Can it move? Is it bigger than a loaf of bread?* Keep a tally of the number of questions asked on the board. Students can all write down their guesses as the 20th question.

3. Show students the turnip. Pass it around the room and elicit words to describe the turnip from the students (e.g., round, smooth, bumpy, heavy).

4. Explain to the students that the story that they are going to read today is about a special turnip. This story originates from Russia. Allow students to explore on a map where Russia is. Support responses with guided questions such as: *Is Russia bigger or smaller than our country? What direction is Russia from where we are now?*

5. Show students the cover of the book *The Giant Turnip*. Ask their predictions about the book using guided questions:
   * *Where do you think this turnip is? Why do you think this?*
   * *How did it get to be so giant?*
   * *Can you think of any other words we could use instead of giant (e.g., enormous, huge, gigantic, massive, large)?*

Vocabulary Development:

6. Engage in vocabulary development with the students using the list of words above or any additional words as you see fit. Using flashcards, pictures, or interactive white-board slides, invite the students to identify, say, use, count syllables, and define the new terms in their own words. You may wish to pre-teach the vocabulary first.

Reading:

7. Ask children's predictions about the book or any connections they may have based on the book's title and cover. Connections may be *text-to-text* (what does the child notice from one book/story to another book/story), *text-to-self* (what does the child notice from the book in relation to his/her own lived experiences), or *text-to-wider-world* (what does the child notice from the book in relation to real world historical or current contexts). Read the blurb at the back of the book to help shape their predictions.

8. Read the book with the children, ideally sitting together so you can show them the pictures while reading. This can be done by conducting a read-aloud, getting the children to read sections after the facilitator (echo reading), all reading it together (choral reading), or reading a sentence each between facilitator and child (see-saw reading). Read with appropriate tone, pace, inflection, and enthusiasm to engage the children as much as possible. If there are children who speak the language of the dual language

book, here would be a nice opportunity to get them to read/translate a section if they would like, or to identify some words they can recognize in the print. In addition, if the PENpal Audio Recorder Pen is available, the children could hear the book read in English or another language.

Discussion to Encourage Reflection and Response:

9. Invite the students to share anything they enjoyed, connected with, didn't understand, or wanted to question through the use of a talking object – the turnip may be used as the talking object if so desired. This can be passed around the circle and only the student who has the talking object may speak, encouraging careful listening and turn-taking skills in the students.

10. Ask a range of literal, inferential, and evaluative questions to gauge comprehension of the text (selected at the discretion of the facilitator):

Literal Questions:

(Readers use information taken directly from the text to answer this type of question.)

  i.   *What was the teacher/adult's name in the story?*
  ii. *Can you list the things that the students planted in the garden?*
  iii. *Who came that allowed the class to pull the turnip out of the ground?*

Inferential Questions:

(Reader must use the information in the text to deduce the answer to this type of question.)

  i. *Why did they plant the turnip seeds in spring?*
  ii. *Why did they decide to go with Samira's idea to pull the turnip out of the ground?*

Evaluative Questions:

(Reader uses their own knowledge to explore answers to this type of question.)

  i.   *What do you think made the turnip so big?*
  ii. *What sort of ways did they use the turnip for the party at the end of the story?*
  iii. *What ways can you think of that they could have used to pull the turnip from the ground?*

Word Identification/Fluency Development:

11. ***Summarizing the Story:*** Break the students into pairs. Challenge the students to see if they can take turns at summarizing the story in one breath. This may take some modeling at a whole-class level a few times first in order for the students to grasp the idea. Scaffold the students to help them realize that they must include the main characters, plot, ending, etc.

12. ***Revisit the Story and Identify Key Vocabulary Words:*** Allow children to revisit some of the vocabulary of the story using the flashcards. For example, the students could reread a section of the story and raise their hands as soon as they hear or see a new vocabulary word, or play language/word games (e.g., charades, hangman/snowman).

Independent Work/Group Work Activity:

13. ***Drama Activity - Recreating the scene from the story:***
The students will (in groups of 3-5) re-enact the scenes from the story. Each child will have to come up with their character's identity and why they think they will be the best at pulling the turnip (e.g., I'm a magician and I can use my magic to make it move, I'm a scientist and I can make a huge lever to pry it out of the ground). The students will perform a brief portion of the story no longer than 3 minutes per group.

14. ***Alternative Drama Activity:***
Allow students to walk around the room. As they are walking, explain that they need the best person possible to come and help pull the turnip out of the ground. Continue to explain that on your signal (e.g., a special word/phrase, a musical chime/sound effect) they will freeze until they are tapped on the shoulder. When they are tapped on the shoulder they must identify who they are and why they would be the best person to pull up the turnip.

15. ***Word Work with Food-Related Words:***
Students can also begin to discover the different words used to describe foods in U.S. and U.K. English through the following activity. On the board, stick up pictures of foods (e.g., turnip/rutabaga, fries/chips, cookie/biscuit). Also place labels that have both the U.S. and U.K. terms for them on the board, jumbled up. Invite students to match the pictures with the U.S. and U.K. terms used to describe the foods. A starting point for this idea can be found here:
- Laliberte, M. (2018) *14 Foods You Didn't Know Were Called by Different Names in the U.K.* Retrieved from https://www.rd.com/food/fun/british-food-names/.

Children can make lists of these words and add to it as a project at home, if so desired. Children who know another language could also add words in their language(s) to provide a greater understanding and appreciation of different languages for the group.

Conclusion:

16. At this point, the facilitator may want to revisit the essential questions to determine whether the children have understood the main ideas of the lesson:
   • *What is the main message of the story of The Giant Turnip?*

   As a concluding consolidation activity, invite the children to discuss these questions with the whole group, in smaller groups, in pairs, or as a written reflection.

Assessment:

Drama as an Assessment Tool: to gauge the student's interpretation and ability to extend their thinking of the story.

Facilitator Observation: of responses to questioning, of drama.

Facilitator questioning: from a range of lower to higher order questions.

Accommodations/Differentiation:

Differential Product/Response:

Ask higher-order thinking questions of the advanced students.

Differential Processes:

• Provide extra wait time and language scaffolds/supports for students who need them (e.g., showing pages from the book, sentence starters).
• Model and support students in the creation of the drama by providing hints and suggestions as to characters they could take on during the scene.
• All students (but especially English language learners, or ELLs) will benefit from pictures accompanying the vocabulary to be learned in the story.
• For ELLs, it may be helpful to allow the child to take home the dual language book either before or after the lesson. It can then be read at home in the home language before class engagement to promote students' confidence in talking about the book in class. If possible, ask the parents to record the book being read in the home language. The book and recording can then be brought into school so that other students can see and hear some of the home languages spoken by their classmates, deepening their appreciation for language diversity.

Extension Activities:

- **Art:** Vegetable printing
- **Music:** Looking at vegetable instruments: https://www.youtube.com/watch?v=b4P3t2nOr00
- **Science:** Plants, growing and changing, the seasons
- **Language Arts:**
    - *"...it was taller than a giraffe, and wider than an elephant."* Exploring similes and other turnip related comparisons (e.g., as heavy as...as round as...).
    - Another option for students is to compile a list of the fairytales and stories that they share in common with one another before beginning this unit. These stories could be re-written by the students and placed together into a folk stories compendium that could be placed in the library.

Vocabulary Flashcards for *The Giant Turnip*:

fruit	weeds	lettuce
vegetables	recovered	helicopter
spring	joy	radish
prepared	suggested	carrot
stronger	enormous	tomato
grabbed	digging	sunflower
frost	planted	pea
strength	wobbled	turnip
rope	feast	bulldozer
raking		

Theme 2:
Folktales, Fables, Myths, and Legends

Topic B:
Legends –
The Children of Lir

Goal: Expose students to a range of traditional literature from different cultures and countries, thereby enabling them to appreciate the multitude of stories told to students around the world.

Language Lizard Book Used: *The Children of Lir*
Retold By Dawn Casey. Illustrated by Diana Mayo.
Available in English with: Albanian, Arabic, Bengali, Chinese, Czech, Farsi, French, German, Irish, Italian, Panjabi, Polish, Portuguese, Somali, Spanish, Tamil, Turkish, Urdu, and Vietnamese.

Snapshot of Lesson:

- Children make **predictions** about the story based on observations.

- Children **"travel thousands of years back in time to Ireland"** to observe the story of *The Children of Lir*.

- Children prepare for their journey by emptying an ancient bowl of **key vocabulary words**.

- Children listen to a **reading of the *story*** of *The Children of Lir*.

- Children **respond to the text** by answering literal, inferential, and evaluative questions.

- In pairs or small groups, children **retell the story** of *The Children of Lir*.

- Children **listen and respond** to *The Children of Lir Overture* composed by the Irish folk group "Loudest Whisper".

- Children **respond to the text** by asking one of the children-swans questions about their experience (Facilitator in Role/Character Hot Seating).

Background Information for Facilitator

Irish Folklore:

There is a strong tradition of storytelling in Ireland. Stories belong to four main categories: The Fenian Cycle, the Ulster Cycle, the Cycle of Kings, and the Mythological Cycle. *The Children of Lir* is part of the Irish Mythological Cycle. Information on the origins of Irish folklore as well as the preservation of Irish folklore can be found on www.askaboutireland.ie (See links below). Some key information related to *The Children of Lir* includes:

1. The *Children of Lir* is an Irish story based on a legend that came to Ireland at the end of the Middle Ages from Britain or France.
2. Lir was a descendant of the Tuatha Dé Danaan (people of the Goddness Danú) tribe who were a supernatural group of people.
3. The lake where Aoife turned the four children into swans is Lake Derravarragh in County Westmeath (East of Ireland, Northeast of Dublin).

4. Inish Glora (the island where the swan-children stayed) is in Erris, Co. Mayo (West coast of Ireland).
5. The Christian Missionary the swan-children met on Inish Glora is believed to be St. Mochaomhóg (St. Moling).

Sources Cited:

- Ask about Ireland. (2008). *The Children of Lir*. Retrieved from http://www.askaboutireland.ie/reading-room/history-heritage/folklore-of-ireland/carlow-folklore/the-story-of-mad-sweeney/the-children-of-lir/

More Information about Irish Folklore and *The Children of Lir*:

- Lysaght, P. (2012). *The Irish mythological cycle*. Retrieved from http://www.askaboutireland.ie/reading-room/history-heritage/folklore-of-ireland/folklore-in-ireland/traditional-storytelling/the-mythological-cycle/the-irish-mythological-cy/
- McGuire, P. (2012). *Feature: Folklore of Ireland*. Retrieved from http://www.askaboutireland.ie/reading-room/history-heritage/folklore-of-ireland/folklore-in-ireland/Introduction/
- *The Children of Lir*. (2008). Retrieved from http://www.askaboutireland.ie/learning-zone/primary-students/looking-at-places/westmeath/the-children-of-lir/

Lesson Plan: *The Children of Lir*

Grade Level: 1-4 (Note: The activities in this lesson plan can be tailored to suit the needs of the specific group that is being taught, at the discretion of the facilitator)

Time Frame: 2 x (45 minute - 1 hour) sessions

Objectives:

Knowledge:

- Identify the origins of the story *The Children of Lir*.
- Learn new vocabulary based on the topic of *The Children of Lir*.

Skills:

- Make predictions based on observations of illustrations.
- Use language to explain and describe.

- Use language to answer and formulate questions.
- Listen and respond to *The Children of Lir Overture*.

Attitudes:

- Understand and appreciate that everyone does not have the same cultural tales and traditional stories around the world by using *The Children of Lir* as an example of a traditional tale from another country.
- Value and respect diversity and lifestyles of others.
- Enjoy listening to the story being read in English and in the other language in the dual language book if possible. The story could be read in a second language with the help of a bilingual parent, child, or teacher, or using the PENpal Audio Recorder Pen.
- Appreciate different languages and scripts around the world.

Essential Questions:

- What is the main message of the story of *The Children of Lir*?

Materials and Resources:

- *The Children of Lir* retold by Dawn Casey.
- Flashcards of key vocabulary words.
- Bowl (for vocabulary words activity – optional).
- *The Children of Lir Overture* (Composed by Irish folk group Loudest Whisper): https://www.youtube.com/watch?v=C5bbZLKoY74
- Piece of clothing (e.g., hat or scarf) for Facilitator in Role/Character Hot Seating activity.
- PENpal Audio Recorder Pen (optional).

Linkage and Integration across subject areas:

Language Arts: Vocabulary development, reading, using language to explain and describe, and using language to formulate and answer questions.

Music: Listen to *The Children of Lir Overture*.

Drama: Role Play (traveling to Ireland), Facilitator in Role/Character Hot Seating activity.

Vocabulary to be Developed in this Lesson:

Key Vocabulary		Story Specific Vocabulary
• children	• yawning	• Lir
• magic	• bathe	• Tuatha Dé Danaan (Two-ha Day Dan-aan)
• king	• shrieking	• Ireland
• queen	• wand	• druid
• wife	• floated	• hypnotic incantation
• stepmother	• terrified	• swan
• sons	• frantically	• curse
• daughters	• cruel	• Irish Sea
• sleepy	• transformed	• Atlantic Ocean
• lake	• fierce	• Sorceress
• lonely	• feathers	• anguish
• bell	• safety	• exile
• wings	• nettles	• Scotland
• music	• tale	• Arctic winds
• palace	• myth	• buffeted
• wedding gift	• legend	• seal
• twins	• holy	• desolate
• heartbroken	• chapel	• fort
• jealous	• radiant	• lament
• dark magic	• ancient	• Inish Glora (In-ish Glore-ah)
		• hermit
		• Sidhe (Irish term for descendants of Tuatha Dé Danaan)
		• seized

Expressions
Her heart grew heavy with hate.
Her voice was as sweet and as thick as honey.
The girl waded in the water.
On a stormy night you can still hear her howls.
He rushed to embrace his children.

Names and Pronunciations of Characters in 'The Children of Lir'
Lir (king), Fionnuala (Fin-OO-la), Aed (Ay), Fiacra (Fee-ak-ra), Conn, Aoife (Ee-fa) the High King's daughter, Bodh the Red (Bov the Red - mighty king of Tuatha Dé Danaan), Evric (farmer), the hermit.

Procedure:

Introduction:

1. Begin the lesson by presenting the cover of the book to the children. Ask the children what they notice about the picture? What is happening in the picture? Encourage the children to explain their responses.

2. Ask the children to use their observations to predict what they think the story will be about.

3. Inform the children that this is a very old story from Ireland.

4. The facilitator may wish to pretend that the group is going to travel back thousands of years to visit Ireland. Ask the children to sit on the floor and to "grab the magic carpet," exclaiming to hold on tight because the group is traveling to Ireland to listen to the story of *The Children of Lir* which took place thousands of years ago.

Vocabulary development:

5. Inform the group that you have an ancient bowl filled with the important words that they will need to learn on their journey to Ireland.

6. Using the list of words tabulated above or any additional words, ask about known vocabulary (key vocabulary /story specific vocabulary) from the story of *The Children of Lir*. This activity can be supported by the use of flashcards and/or pictures.

7. Present new vocabulary (key vocabulary /story specific vocabulary) to the children. Using flashcards and/or pictures, invite the children to say/read each word. Ask the children if they know the meanings of the words and encourage them to provide explanations of the words if possible. The facilitator may need to elaborate or provide additional explanations of some words and say the words in sentences so the students can hear the words in context. The facilitator may ask the children to create their own sentences containing the words, encouraging the children to make personal connections with the words. If there are bilingual children in the group, it may be possible to ask them to say the words in their language(s).

Reading:

8. Read the book *The Children of Lir* with the children. The facilitator may choose to read the book aloud to the children, engage in choral reading (facilitator and children read the story together in unison), or see-saw reading (facilitator reads one sentence, children read the following sentence and continue alternating reading after each

sentence). It is important to read with appropriate tone, pace, inflection, and expression to engage the children as much as possible. If there are children who speak the language of the dual language book, here would be a nice opportunity to ask them to read/translate a section of the story if they would like. Moreover, if the facilitator has a PENpal Audio Recorder device, the children could listen to a reading of the story in English or the other language of the dual language book.

9. Throughout the story, explicitly draw children's attention to the illustrations to promote comprehension of the text.

10. During reading, encourage children to make connections (orally, using mime, in writing). Connections may be *text-to-self* (what does the child notice from the book in relation to his/her own lived experiences), *text-to-text* (what does the child notice from one book/story to another book/story), *or text-to-wider-world* (what does the child notice from the book in relation to real world historical or current contexts).

Discussion to Encourage Reflection and Response:

11. Facilitate discussion with the group of children using literal, inferential, and evaluative questions. The facilitator may wish to select questions from the following list:

Literal Questions:

(Readers use information directly from the text to answer this type of question.)

   i.   *How many children did the king, Lir, have?*
   ii. *What animal did Aoife (the children's stepmother) turn the children into?*
   iii. *In what three locations did the swan-children have to live according to the curse?*

Inferential Questions:

(Reader must use the information in the text to deduce the answer.)

   i. *Why did Lir return day after day to listen to four swans singing?*
   ii. *Why did the swans sing a lament when they flew over the land of their childhood?*

Evaluative Questions:

(Reader uses his/her own knowledge to explore answers to this type of question.)

   i. *Do you think it was fair for Aoife to turn the children into swans? Why or why not?*

    ii. *How to do you think Fionnuala, Aed, Fiacra, and Conn felt when they transformed from swans into old, withered people?*

Word Identification/Fluency Development:

12. ***Revisit the story and identify key vocabulary words:*** Display key vocabulary words from the story. Reread a section from the story and ask the children to raise their hands when they hear or see one of the key vocabulary words.

13. ***Retell the story (in pairs or small groups):*** Present key words from the story listed in order as they appear in the story. Using the words, children retell the story in small groups or pairs. The facilitator may ask the children to retell the story orally or in writing. The facilitator may present sentences with key words for this activity to provide the children with additional support. The children could also retell the story using illustrations, mime, or still images.

Independent Work/Group Work Activity:

14. ***Listen to The Children of Lir Overture (by Irish folk group Loudest Whisper):***
    - Before playing *The Children of Lir Overture* to the children, inform the group that you will play a piece of music to them and that you would like them to listen carefully. Tell the children that you would like them to try to identify the instruments they hear playing (flute, drums, string instruments, pipes, guitar, voice). Ask the children what they notice about the tempo of the music? Is the tempo fast or slow? Does the tempo stay the same?
    - Inform the children that *The Children of Lir Overture* will be played another time. Ask the children to consider which parts of the story *The Children of Lir* are being told at different points during the piece of music. Displaying pictures or key words from the story *The Children of Lir* would support children carrying out this activity. Additionally, the children could use the pictures to make a storyboard to illustrate *The Children of Lir Overture*.

15. ***Facilitator in Role & Hot Seating Drama Activity:***
    - A piece of clothing (e.g., hat or scarf) will be needed for this activity in order to signify that the facilitator will assume the role of Fionnuala, Aed, Fiacra, or Conn from the story.
    - Preparation for Facilitator in Role: Ask the children to consider what they would ask the children of Lir about their lives if they could meet the characters from the story. A "Think-Pair-Share" activity may be useful to help the children formulate questions to ask the characters.
    - Facilitator in Role: After the children have shared their questions with the whole group, inform the children that when the facilitator is wearing the piece of clothing (i.e., hat or scarf), they will assume the role of Fionnuala, Aed, Fiacra, or Conn.

- Character Hot Seating: Wearing the piece of clothing, thank the children for coming to Ireland to speak to them. Next, invite the children to ask questions they devised about the story *The Children of Lir*. At the end of this activity, the facilitator will remove the piece of clothing used to signify that he/she has returned from the role of Fionnuala, Aed, Fiacra, or Conn.

Conclusion:

Facilitate a discussion with the group. Ask the children to explain what they learned about the story of *The Children of Lir*. At this point, the facilitator may want to revisit essential question to determine whether the children have understood the main idea of the lesson:

- *What is a main message of the story of The Children of Lir?*

As a concluding activity, invite the children to discuss these questions with the whole group, in smaller groups, in pairs, as a written reflection. An activity such as "Two Stars and a Wish" may be a nice conclusion to the lesson. In pairs, children say two things they have learned and one thing they would like to learn about *The Children of Lir*.

Assessment:

Facilitator Observation: Children's engagement and interaction with the lesson, engagement in discussions, and engagement with facilitator designed tasks.

Facilitator Questioning: Higher and lower order questioning (i.e., literal, inferential, and evaluative questions).

Facilitator Designed Tasks: Making predictions, vocabulary games, reading fluency activities, listening and responding to music, and drama activity (character hot-seating).

Self-Assessment: "Two Stars and a Wish"

Accommodations/Differentiation:

Differential modes of Representation:

Photos, pictures, flashcards, *The Children of Lir Overture* (music), drama.

Differential Questioning:

Use of higher and lower order questioning (i.e., literal, inferential, and evaluative questions).

Differential Product/Response:

Written responses, oral responses, music responses *to The Children of Lir Overture*, drama responses.

In a classroom setting, it may be helpful for the English language learners (ELLs) to take the dual language book home either before or after the lesson. The ELL student may read the book at home in the language spoken by his/her family. This will increase the child's confidence when talking about the book in school. If possible, ask the child's parent/guardian to read and record the book in the language that he/she speaks at home. The recording could then be played in the classroom, enabling children to hear other languages spoken by their peers at home.

Extension Activities:

Still Images/Freeze Frame (Drama Exercise):

The facilitator may wish to extend children's engagement with *The Children of Lir* through still imagery activities. In groups, the children can act as characters such as the swan-children from the story and create a still image (freeze frame) depicting a scene or key moment from the story. If there is a large group of children carrying out this exercise, each group may present its still image to the whole the group. The facilitator may wish to tap one of the students creating the still image on the shoulder and ask the children in the large group questions such as:

i.   *What do you think this character is looking at?*
ii. *What do you think this character is doing?*
iii. *How do you think this character is reacting?*
iv. *Does any tension exist between the characters?*
v.   *What do you think will happen next?*

Character Sketch (English Writing):

Through questioning and discussion, ask the children what they know about the main characters in the story (e.g., Fionnuala, King Lir, the stepmother Queen Aoife, the hermit). Discuss attributes such as appearance, role in the story, and dealing with other characters. Inform the children that they will create a character profile of one of the characters in the story. To help children generate ideas for this activity, the facilitator may ask the children to close their eyes and visualize the character they have chosen. Next, ask children to draw a sketch of their chosen character. Finally, encourage the children to write adjectives or vocabulary words to describe the character.

Drawing 'photographs' taken on journey to Ireland (Visual Arts):

Engage in a discussion with the children, asking them to describe what they saw on their "visit" to Ireland. Ask the children to identify key moments from the story (e.g., King Lir marrying Queen Aoife, the children swimming in the lake, Queen Aoife casting a spell on the children, the children turning into swans, King Lir striking Queen Aoife with his Druid's wand, King Lir listening to the swans singing, the swans flying to the Irish Sea, the swans flying to the Atlantic Sea, the swans meeting the hermit, the swans turning into old people after the bell rings). Inform the children that they will be creating a photograph to illustrate a key moment they observed from their "visit." Ask the children to engage in a Think/Pair/Share activity to discuss possible ideas to draw in their photograph.

Provide the children with coloring materials to carry out the activity. The facilitator may wish to provide children with a simple template (e.g., a rectangular outline bordering page to indicate that the drawing is a photograph). While the children draw the photographs, the facilitator may circulate around the room, offering assistance, providing descriptive feedback, and making suggestions to the children. When the children have finished creating their photographs, ask the children to present their completed artworks to the group. Encourage the children to explain what key moment they chose to draw and why they chose to draw that particular moment from the story.

Project Work on Ireland (Geography):

Develop the children's map reading skills by locating Ireland on a map. Using a large poster/chart, a digital map, or an atlas, ask the children questions to encourage them to examine the physical features of the country. For example, what continent is Ireland in? What countries (if any) border Ireland? Is Ireland an island country? What sea borders Ireland? What seas were mentioned in the story (e.g., Irish Sea, Atlantic Sea)? Ask the children to name and locate main cities, rivers, and mountains in Ireland.

Additionally, children could conduct independent research on Ireland. Areas of focus for this project work may include:

- **General Information:** Population, capital city, government, language(s), predominant religion, currency, national symbol.
- **Map of Ireland:** Indicate physical features such as capital city, bordering seas, islands, mountain ranges, rivers, and lakes. Note interesting facts about the country's geography (e.g., longest river, highest mountain, largest island).
- **Flag of Ireland:** Picture/sketch of the flag and information about the flag.
- **Language & Culture:** Identify the language(s) spoken in the country with examples of every day phrases. Identify some of the country's art and culture, customs and traditions, traditional dances, and sports.

- **Traditional Food:** Identify examples of traditional dishes, briefly explaining the ingredients.
- **Attractions:** Identify interesting places to visit, tourist attractions, briefly describe the places.
- **Interesting Facts:** Create a "Did you know?" page with some interesting facts learned about the country (e.g., identify a famous person who was born in Ireland).
- **Craft:** Make a craft/item to represent something from the country's culture. For example, make a traditional dish or construct a famous landmark.
- **Similarities and Differences:** Children identify similarities and differences between Ireland and where they live or their countries of birth.

Vocabulary Flashcards for *The Children of Lir:*

Lir	Ireland	druid
swan	curse	palace
exile	fort	lament
hermit	twins	heartbroken
jealous	dark magic	yawning
bathe	shrieking	terrified

frantically	cruel	transformed
fierce	feathers	safety
nettles	tale	myth
legend	holy	chapel
radiant	ancient	king
queen	stepmother	bell

Theme 2:
Folktales, Fables, Myths, and Legends

Topic C:
Folktales –
Yeh-Hsien a Chinese Cinderella

Goal: Expose students to a range of traditional literature from different cultures and countries, thereby enabling them to appreciate the multitude of stories told to students around the world.

Book Used in Lesson: *Yeh-Hsien a Chinese Cinderella*
Retold by Dawn Casey. Illustrated by Richard Holland.
Available In English with: Albanian, Arabic, Bengali, Chinese, Farsi, French, Gujarati, Hindi, Japanese, Kurdish, Panjabi, Polish, Portuguese, Russian, Somali, Spanish, Swedish, Tagalog, Tamil, Turkish, Urdu, and Vietnamese.

Snapshot of Lesson:

- **Retelling** the story of Cinderella that they are familiar with in a circle.

- Children **explore key vocabulary** from the story of *Yeh-Hsien a Chinese Cinderella*, **predict** what the story will be about, and **make connections** with the story.

- Children **read** the story of *Yeh-Hsien a Chinese Cinderella* with the facilitator.

- Engage in **discussion** about the story with the children.

- Using **art** to design a new dress for Yeh-Hsien to wear to the Spring Festival.

Background Information for Facilitator

It is important that the facilitator makes students aware of the difference between folktales, fables, myths, and legends. Further information can be found here:

- East of England Broadband Network. (2006). *Teachers' resources: What are myths, legends and folktales?* Retrieved from http://myths.e2bn.org/teacher/adults/info311-what-are-myths-legends-and-folktales.html
- Andie Worsley. (2017). *Traditional Literature: Folktales, Fairytales, and Fables.* Retrieved from https://www.youtube.com/watch?v=eaVh8yGbXNc

This story originated in China. It is said to be the oldest known version of the Cinderella story, dating back to between 618 and 907 A.D. The facilitator may wish to read a different version either before or after this adapted version and encourage the students to note the similarities and differences between the versions, commenting on why they think certain changes were made and other elements of the story were kept. More information about other versions of the Cinderella story from around the world can be found at:

- Rachel Hope Crossman. (2011). *365 Cinderellas.* Retrieved from http://www.365cinderellas.com/p/cool-cinderella-stories.html
- Fairytalez. (2016). *Cinderella Tales: 10 International Versions of the Beloved Tale.* Retrieved from https://fairytalez.com/blog/cinderella-international-versions/

It may be a good idea to pre-teach the students the new vocabulary in the story first so that they are able to focus on the reading and content of the book during this lesson.

Lesson Plan: *Yeh-Hsien a Chinese Cinderella*

Grade Level: K-4 (Note: The activities in this lesson plan can be tailored to suit the needs of the specific group that is being taught, at the discretion of the facilitator.)

Time Frame: 30-40 minute session.

Objectives:

Knowledge:

- Identify the origins of the story of *Yeh-Hsien a Chinese Cinderella*.
- List some of the versions of the Cinderella story they have heard growing up.

Skills:

- Identify, define, and use the new vocabulary in the story.
- Enhance their comprehension strategies using literal, inferential, and evaluative questioning.
- Practice their summarization skills using the story as an anchor text.
- Explore the alternative languages of the text for similarities and differences.
- Discuss and explain how this adapted version of the story differs from the original version.

Attitudes:

- Understand and appreciate that everyone does not have the same cultural tales and traditional stories around the world by using *Yeh-Hsien a Chinese Cinderella* as an example of a traditional tale from another country.

Essential Questions:

- What is the main message of the story of *Yeh-Hsien a Chinese Cinderella*?

Materials and Resources:

- *Yeh-Hsien a Chinese Cinderella* by Dawn Casey.
- New vocabulary flashcards.
- Talking object (e.g., ball) to signify whose turn it is to talk during discussion.
- Range of art materials (e.g., watercolors, acrylic paints, chalks, fabrics, textured materials, paper).

Linkage and Integration Across Subject Areas:

Language Arts/Reading: Engaging with literature.

Geography: Locating where in the world the story originates.

Visual Art: Creating a Cinderella dress.

Vocabulary to be Developed in Lesson:

Key Vocabulary		Story Specific Vocabulary
• pebbles • dazzling • shimmered • festival • tremble • tender • spiced • beamed • puzzled • frown • bare • snort • beaded • dew • mist • glitter • neighbouring/ neighboring • exquisite • marveled • kingdom • vowed • declared • wayside • hollered • heavenly • innermost • agape	• sorrow • hardly • scrap • firewood • nourished • thrust • thrashed • crooned • wretched • plunged • dagger • gloated • flesh • glinting • weeping • wailing • crumpled • brow • reddened • coarse • compassion • grant • precious • scent • determined • hammered	• southern • stepmother • scroll • Yeh-Hsien • tatters and rags • fins • grains of rice • clump of reeds • tattered • ragged • ducked • dung heap • jade • moon pearls • plum blossom • honour/honor • ancestors • robe of silk • kingfisher feathers • indigo • lapis • turquoise • willow • stepsister • To'han • gongs • delicacies

Procedure:

Introduction:

1. To get the children thinking about the version of the Cinderella story with which they are familiar, ask them to get together in a circle. Explain that you are going to tell the story of Cinderella together as a group. Invite them to pause for a moment and think about answering the important questions (i.e., who, what, where, when, why, and how) when telling the story to someone who has never heard it before. A talking object, such as a ball, may be passed from person to person in order or thrown randomly among the group whenever a student has something to add.

2. Invite children to think about where they heard their version from – family, movies, books, etc. Ask children if they noticed whether any detail they heard another child say differed from their version of the story.

3. Allow children to return to their places. Explain to the children that the group will be reading a version of the Cinderella story that they may not have heard before. Tell them that it comes from China. Allow students to explore on a map where China is. Support responses with guiding questions (e.g., Is China bigger or smaller than where we are now? What direction is China from where we are now?)

4. Show students the cover of the book *Yeh-Hsien a Cinderella Story*. Ask their predictions about the book using guiding questions:
   - *Looking at just the picture, what parts of the story do you think are the same/different to your version? (e.g., stepsisters, party, fancy clothes)*
   - *Which character do you think is Yeh-Hsien? Why do you think that?*

Vocabulary Development:

5. Engage in vocabulary development with the students using the list of words above or any additional words as you see fit. Using flashcards, pictures, or interactive whiteboard slides, invite the students to identify, say, use, count syllables, and define the new terms in their own words. You may wish to pre-teach the vocabulary first.

Reading:

6. Ask the children's predictions about the book or any connections they may have based on the book's title and cover. Connections may be *text-to-text* (what does the child notice from one book/story to another book/story), *text-to-self* (what does the child notice from the book in relation to his/her own lived experiences), or *text-to-wider-world* (what does the child notice from the book in relation to real world historical or current contexts). Read the blurb at the back of the book to help shape their predictions.

7. Read the book with the children, ideally sitting together so you can show them the pictures while reading. This can be done by conducting a read-aloud, getting the children to read sections after the facilitator (echo reading), all reading it together (choral reading), or reading a sentence each between facilitator and child (see-saw reading). Read with appropriate tone, pace, inflection, and enthusiasm to engage the children as much as possible. If there are children who speak the language of the dual language book, here would be a nice opportunity to get them to read/translate a section if they would like, or to identify some words they can recognize in the print. In addition, if the PENpal Audio Recorder Pen is available, the children could hear the book read in English or another language.

Discussion to Encourage Reflection and Response:

8. Invite the students to share anything they enjoyed, connected with, didn't understand, or wanted to question through the use of a talking object. This can be passed around the circle and only the student who has the talking object may speak, encouraging careful listening and turn-taking skills in the students.

9. Ask a range of literal, inferential, and evaluative questions to gauge comprehension of the text (selected at the discretion of the facilitator):

Literal Questions:

(Readers use information taken directly from the text to answer this type of question.)

    i. *What did the fish look like?*
    ii. *Where were the fish bones hidden by the stepmother?*
    iii. *What marked the arrival of spring?*
    iv. *What were some of the colors of Yeh-Hsien's kingfisher dress?*

Inferential Questions:

(Reader must use the information in the text to deduce the answer to this type of question.)

    i. *Why do you think that Yeh-Hsien's stepmother said that the fish tasted "twice as good as an ordinary fish"?*
    ii. *Why did Yeh-Hsien and the king bury the fish bones?*

Evaluative Questions:

(Reader uses their own knowledge to explore answers to this type of question.)

    i. *Why do you think Yeh-Hsien's stepmother said that she deserved a new dress?*

ii. *Who was the old man that came to visit Yeh-Hsien?*

iii. *Why would people gather to honor their ancestors at the Spring Festival?*

iv. *What idea would you have come up with to find the owner of the shoe?*

Word identification/Fluency Development:

10. **Summarizing the story:** Break the students into pairs. Challenge the students to see if they can take turns at summarizing the story in one breath. This may take some modeling at a whole-class level a few times first in order for the students to grasp the idea. Scaffold the students to help them realize that they must include the main characters, plot, ending, etc.

11. **Revisit the story and identify key vocabulary words:** Allow children to revisit some of the vocabulary of the story using the flashcards. For example, the students could reread a section of the story and raise their hands as soon as they hear or see a new vocabulary word, or play language/word games (e.g., charades, hangman/snowman).

Independent Work/Group Work Activity:

12. **Art activity:** Show children the page where Yeh-Hsien is wearing the Kingfisher Dress. Recall the different shades of blue in the dress with the children. They may wish to use similar shades of blue, make up their own shades of blue, or use a completely new set of colors to create their own dresses for Yeh-Hsien to wear to the Spring Festival. Children can use a variety of mediums (e.g., acrylic paints, watercolors, chalks, fabrics, textured materials) in their creations, which can be explored in 2D or 3D forms. Encourage children to seek inspiration from colors/textures they may have noticed in nature to be incorporated into their design. Children may wish to plan their design roughly first before they decide on their design.

When completed, the children can put on a mini fashion show of their designs for one another. Encourage the other children to comment on things they like about their classmate's designs. Model this process beforehand by taking some children's designs as examples (e.g., I like how X used a variety of textures in his/her design. This makes it very eye-catching)

Conclusion:

13. At this point, the facilitator may want to revisit the essential question to determine whether the children have understood the main ideas of the lesson:
    • What do you think is the main message of the story of *Yeh-Hsien a Chinese Cinderella*?

As a concluding consolidation activity, invite the children to discuss these questions with the whole group, in smaller groups, in pairs, or as a written reflection.

Assessment:

Art as an Assessment Tool: to gauge the student's interpretation and ability to extend their thinking of the story.

Facilitator Observation: of responses to questioning, of drama.

Facilitator Questioning: from a range of lower to higher order questions.

Accommodations/Differentiation:

Differential Product/Response:

Ask higher-order thinking questions of the advanced students.

Differential Processes:

- Provide extra wait time and language scaffolds/supports for students who need them (e.g., showing pages from the book, sentence starters).
- Model and support students in the creation of the drama by providing hints and suggestions as to characters they could take on during the scene.
- All students (but especially English language learners, or ELLs) will benefit from pictures accompanying the vocabulary to be learned in the story.
- For ELLs, it may be helpful to allow the child to take home the dual language book either before or after the lesson. It can then be read at home in the home language before class engagement to promote students' confidence in talking about the book in class. If possible, ask the parents to record the book being read in the home language. The book and recording can then be brought into school so that other students can see and hear some of the home languages spoken by their classmates, deepening their appreciation for language diversity.

Extension Activities:

- **Music:** Exploring traditional Chinese music (that may be played at Spring Festivals)
- **Geography:** Exploring Spring Festivals in China and around the World
- **Science:** Life cycle of fish, homes, and habitats
- **Language Arts:** Another option is for students to compile a list of the fairytales and stories that they share in common with one another before beginning this unit. These stories could be re-written by the students and placed together into a folk stories compendium that could be placed in the library.

Vocabulary Flashcards for *Yeh-Hsien a Chinese Cinderella:*

southern	sorrow	stepmother
hardly	scroll	scrap
Yeh-hsien	firewood	tatters and rags
nourished	fins	grains of rice
pebbles	thrust	clump of reeds
thrashed	tattered	crooned
ragged	wretched	ducked
dung heap	jade	plunged
moon pearls	dagger	plum blossom

honour/ honor	gloated	ancestors
flesh	robe of silk	kingfisher feathers
glinting	indigo	weeping
lapis	wailing	turquoise
crumpled	willow	brow
stepsister	reddened	To'han
coarse	compassion	gongs
grant	delicacies	precious
scent	sighed	determined
dazzling	shimmered	festival

tremble	tender	spiced
beamed	puzzled	frown
bare	snort	beaded
dew	mist	glitter
neighbouring/ neighboring	exquisite	marveled
kingdom	vowed	declared
wayside	hollered	innermost
agape	heavenly	

Theme 3:
Holidays and Festivals

Topic A:
Chinese New Year –
Li's Chinese New Year

Goal: Provide children with opportunities to learn about and appreciate a range of holidays and festivals celebrated around the world.

Book Used in Lesson: *Li's Chinese New Year*
Written by Fang Wang. Illustrated by Jennifer Corfield.
Available in English with: Arabic, Chinese, French, Japanese, Polish, Portuguese, Spanish, Tagalog, Urdu, and Vietnamese.

Snapshot of Lesson:

- Using a picture of the 12 zodiac animals from the opening pages of *Li's Chinese New Year*, children **identify** the animals and **predict** the significance of the animals to the story.

- A parcel addressed to the group containing key vocabulary from the story of *Li's Chinese New Year* arrives. Children **explore key vocabulary** from the story.

- Children listen to a **reading of the story** of *Li's Chinese New Year*.

- Children **respond to the text** by answering literal, inferential, and evaluative questions.

- Children **retell the story** in pairs or small groups.

- Children **create a dragon as a group** using a large strip of fabric.

- Children **create and perform a Dragon Dance** movement as a group.

Background Information for Facilitator

Chinese New Year:

Chinese New Year is a public holiday in China. Commonly known as Spring Festival, the holiday is set according to the lunar calendar. Therefore, the date changes from year to year (it usually falls between mid-January and mid-February). Some of the traditions many people in China follow during Chinese New Year include:

- Fireworks displays
- Parades
- Dragon dance performances (to bring luck in the new year)
- Feasts
- Children receive gifts including red envelopes with money and new clothes

Legends Underpinning *Li's Chinese New Year*:

The book *Li's Chinese New Year* contains information about Chinese mythology regarding the origins of the Chinese Zodiac. Legends underpinning the celebration of Chinese New Year, including *The Monster Nian*, *The Great Race,* and *The Emperor's Feast,* are embedded in the book. Summaries of these stories, adapted from the audio of the book, are included below. The facilitator may play these stories with the PENpal Audio Recorder Pen or simply share the narratives.

The Monster Nian:

There was a man-eating wild monster called Nian. This monster had an extremely large mouth and was able to swallow several people in a single bite. At the beginning of winter, the monster attacked villages and ate whatever it could. These villages lived in terror over the winter. Some people would take young children into forests to hide from Nian. However, on one occasion a wise old man told an old woman, "I will teach you how to scare Nian away." That evening, when Nian arrived at the village he saw that all the houses were empty except for one house, where the old woman lived. As Nian approached the house, there was a deafening noise caused by fireworks. The fireworks lit up the house which was completely covered in red paper. Nian was terrified and fled back into the sea. The villagers returned and saw that the old woman was unharmed. When the villagers knew that the monster was afraid of loud noises and the color red, they decided that at the end of winter they would start a fire in front of every door, stay awake, and make as much noise as they could. The following year, the villagers were ready for the monster. They set off fireworks, lit lamps, and decorated their houses in red. They painted red paper on the doors, wore red clothing, hung up red lanterns, made loud music, played the gong and drums, danced, and burned fireworks whenever Nian was about to arrive to scare the beast away. Nian never bothered them again. Ever since, this has been a tradition in China. It is a celebration of another safe year ahead.

The Great Race:

The Story of the Chinese Horoscopes began when Jade Emperor announced to the entire animal kingdom that there would be an amazing race. The first 12 animals to cross the finish line would each be awarded one year in the lunar calendar. Cat and Rat were the best of friends and both decided to take part in the race. Running very quickly, Cat and Rat took the lead. However, they came to a river with a very strong current. Cat and Rat could not swim across. As Ox's eyesight was very poor, Rat suggested to Ox that they would help each other. Cat and Rat sat on Ox's back to get across the river. Rat was very determined to win so Rat pushed Cat off Ox. Cat fell into the river. Rat leaped off Ox's back when they reached the shore and crossed the finish line. The Jade Emperor rewarded Rat with the first spot. These animals were each awarded a year in the lunar calendar:

101

i. Rat
ii. Ox
iii. Tiger
iv. Rabbit
v. Dragon
vi. Snake
vii. Horse
viii. Sheep
ix. Monkey
x. Rooster
xi. Dog
xii. Pig

After congratulating all twelve animals, the Jade Emperor thanked Cat for joining the race but he was just too late. Cat swore that Cat and Rat would be enemies forever.

The Emperor's Feast:

Before Jade Emperor passed away, the emperor summoned all the creatures in his kingdom for a great feast. Expecting the whole animal kingdom to attend, great preparations were made. However, only twelve animals came to bid him farewell. Emperor was sad and angry that the other animals did not come to join him but he did not punish them. Instead, he rewarded the twelve animals that were loyal. He did this by naming a year after them so that they would be remembered as special forever.

Animal	Year
Dragon	2000, 2012, 2024
Snake	2001, 2013, 2025
Horse	2002, 2014, 2026
Sheep	2003, 2015, 2027
Monkey	2004, 2016, 2028
Rooster	2005, 2017, 2029
Dog	2006, 2018, 2030
Pig	2007, 2019, 2031
Rat	2008, 2020, 2032
Ox	2009, 2021, 2033
Tiger	2010, 2022, 2034
Rabbit	2011, 2023, 2035

Sources:

- CultureGrams World Edition. (2014). *People's Republic of China*. Retrieved from https://www.gvsu.edu/cms4/asset/7D7DCFF8-C4AD-66A3-6344C7E690C4BFD9/china_2014.pdf
- PENpal Audio Recorder Pen audio recording in Wang, F., & Corfield, J. (Illustrator). (2010). Li's Chinese New Year. London, UK: Mantra Lingua Ltd.

Lesson Plan: *Li's Chinese New Year*

Grade Level: 3-5 (Note: The activities in this lesson plan can be tailored to suit the needs of the specific group that is being taught, at the discretion of the facilitator.)

Time Frame: 2 x (45 minute - 1 hour) sessions.

Objectives:

Knowledge:

- Learn that there are zodiac animals associated with each year.
- Learn that there are 12 zodiac animals in total.
- Learn new vocabulary based on the topic of Chinese New Year.
- Learn about traditional customs and practices during Chinese New Year celebrations.
- Learn about the origin of Chinese New Year (mythology underpinning the festival).

Skills:

- Listen to the story of *Li's Chinese New Year*.
- Use language to explain and describe.
- Make predictions based on observations of illustrations.
- Create a dragon as a group.
- Create a dragon dance movement as a group.

Attitudes:

- Appreciate traditional customs and practices during Chinese New Year celebrations.
- Appreciate the importance of Chinese New Year to communities around the world.
- Value and respect diversity and lifestyles of others.

- Enjoy listening to the story being read in English and in the other language of the dual language book if possible. The story could be read in a second language with the help of a bilingual parent, child, or teacher, or using the PENpal Audio Recorder Pen.
- Appreciate different languages and scripts from around the world.

Essential Questions:

- How is Chinese New Year celebrated?
- What customs followed by Li are similar/different to customs celebrated in your home?
- For those children who do not celebrate Chinese New Year, how are some traditions of *Li's Chinese New Year* similar/different to holidays they celebrate in the winter? What traditions do they have around meal times, gift giving, and celebrations?

Materials and Resources:

- *Li's Chinese New Year* by Fang Wang.
- Flashcards of key vocabulary words.
- Parcel addressed to the group containing flashcards with vocabulary words (optional).
- Video of a dragon dance.
- Art materials for making a group dragon: Fabric (long enough for all children to stand under in line), pieces of fabric/material, colored card, scissors, coloring markers/pencils/paint, glue, tape, string.
- Suitable music for Dragon Dance movement.
- PENpal Audio Recorder Pen (optional).

Linkage and Integration Across Subject Areas:

Language Arts: Vocabulary development, reading, using language to explain and describe.

Art: Create a dragon as a group.

Drama/Movement: Create a dragon dance movement as a group.

Vocabulary to be Developed in Lesson:

Key Vocabulary		Story Specific Vocabulary
• China	• ox	• Chinese new year
• animal	• cousin	• Chinese zodiac
• colorful	• born	• cobra
• mask	• rat	• Nian (monster)
• shiny	• finishing line	• New Year's parade
• lion	• cheating	• New Year's banners
• snake	• charming	• bad spirits
• hood	• dishes	• lanterns
• dog	• coin	• dumpling
• monkey	• packet	• steamed bread
• tiger	• even number	• lamb rolls
• hail	• new baby	• meat stuffing
• rabbit	• volunteers	• "kung hei fat choi" (happy new year/con-
• chicken	• good/bad luck	gratulations and be prosperous)
• pig	• cunning	• Emperor's feast
• assembly	• charming	• lucky coin
• celebrate	• graceful	• new year's celebrations
• dragon	• elegant	• kalends (the first day of the new year)
• fireworks	• paper cutouts	• new beginnings
• school parade	• firework display	• lucky sign
	• New Year's Eve	• dragon dancers

Expressions

Secretly he was a bit disappointed.

Chen said under his breath so that Mum couldn't hear.

Granny has sent beautiful lanterns and paper cotouts all the way from China.

Li's stomach growled. Li ate until he thought he would burst.

The family wrapped up warn.

Procedure:

Introduction:

1. Begin lesson by presenting the double page spread from the book *Li's Chinese New Year*:

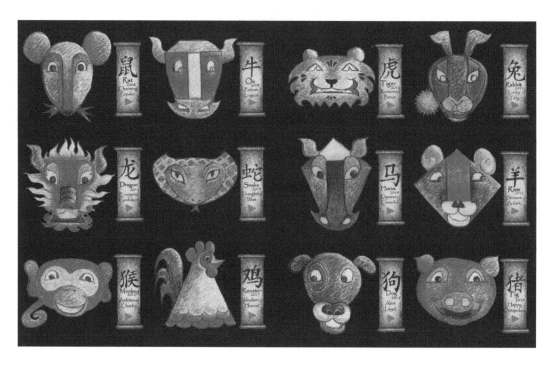

2. Ask the children how many animals are in the picture and whether they can name them all. Inform the children that the animals are the zodiac animals, which are important for the celebration of Chinese New Year. Inform the group that they are going to find out why these twelve animals are the zodiac signs.

3. Ask children to predict the significance of the twelve zodiac animals to the story *Li's Chinese New Year*.

Vocabulary Development:

4. Inform the children that a parcel addressed to the group arrived containing important words that they will need to learn before reading the story.

5. Using the list of words tabulated above or any additional words, elicit known vocabulary (key vocabulary/story specific vocabulary) on the topic of Chinese New Year. This activity can be supported by the use of flashcards and/or pictures.

6. Present new vocabulary (key vocabulary /story specific vocabulary) to the children. Using flashcards and/or pictures, invite the children to say/read each word. Ask the children if they know the meanings of the words and encourage them to provide explanations of the words if possible. The facilitator may need to elaborate or provide additional explanations of some words and say the words in sentences so the students can hear the words in context. The facilitator may ask the children to create their own sentences containing the words, encouraging the children to make personal connections

with the words. If there are bilingual children in the group, it may be possible to ask them to say the words in their language(s).

Reading:

7. Read the book *Li's Chinese New Year* with the children. The facilitator may choose to read the book aloud to the children, engage in choral reading (facilitator and children read the story together in unison), or see-saw reading (facilitator reads one sentence, children read the following sentence and continue alternating reading after each sentence). It is important to read with appropriate tone, pace, inflection, and expression to engage the children as much as possible. If there are children who speak the language of the dual language book, here would be a nice opportunity to ask them to read/translate a section of the story if they would like. Moreover, if the facilitator has a PENpal Audio Recorder Pen, the children could listen to a reading of the story in English or the other language of the dual language book.

8. Throughout the story, explicitly draw children's attention to the illustrations to promote comprehension of the text.

9. Encourage children to make connections (orally, using mime, in writing). Connections may be *text-to-self* (what does the child notice from the book in relation to his/her own lived experiences), *text-to-text* (what does the child notice from one book/story to another book/story), or *text-to-wider-world* (what does the child notice from the book in relation to real world historical or current contexts).

Discussion to Encourage Reflection and Response:

10. Facilitate discussion with the group of children using literal, inferential, and evaluative questions. The facilitator may wish to select questions from the following list:

Literal Questions:

(Readers use information directly from the text to answer this type of question.)

   i. *How many animals are illustrated at the bottom of the first page of Li's Chinese New Year? Can you name them?*
   ii. *Who does Li say will be a strong ox?*
   iii. *What did Granny send from China?*
   iv. *What story did Grandpa tell Li and Chen on New Year's Eve?*
   v. *What was in the two small red packets?*
   vi. *What animal was Li and Chen's newborn cousin?*

Inferential Questions:

(Reader must use the information in the text to deduce the answer.)

   i. *Why do you think Grandpa says that Rat has all the best qualities?*
   ii. *Why do you think the packets were red?*
   iii. *Why is Li and Chen's newborn cousin an ox?*

Evaluative Questions:

(Reader uses his/her own knowledge to explore answers to this type of question.)

   i. *Do you think the class enjoyed watching the video of the lion dancers? Why/Why not?*
   ii. *Do you think Li is happy with Miss Green's plan at the end of the story? Why/Why not?*

Word Identification/Fluency Development:

11. **Revisit the Story and Identify Key Vocabulary Words:** Display key vocabulary words from the story. Reread a section from the story and ask the children to raise their hands when they hear or see one of the key vocabulary words.

12. **Retell the Story:** Present key words from the story listed in order as they appear in the story. Using the words, children retell the story in small groups or pairs. The facilitator may ask the children to retell the story orally or in writing. The facilitator may present sentences with key words for this activity to provide the children with additional support. The children could also retell the story using illustrations, mime or still images.

Independent Work/Group Work Activity:

13. **Whole Group Art & Movement Exercise:**
   • Watch a video of a dragon dance with the children. Ask the children about the movement of the dragon, what do they notice? Elicit from the children that each person copies the actions of the person in front of him or her. Draw the children's attention to the leader of the parade who carries a sphere. This sphere represents the sun. Many people believe that the dragon is chasing the sun. In the dance, the dragon's head follows the movement of the sphere.
   • Inform the children that they will make a dragon together as a group using a long strip of fabric. Then they will create a dragon dance together.
   • Lay the fabric on the floor and ask the children to sit along the length of the fabric. Each child will decorate an area of the fabric using scrap materials, colored paper, crepe paper, colored markers, and embellishments. The facilitator may ask the children to work together to create the dragon's head (eyes, teeth, etc.) and/or a

sun to lead the dance. The children may have additional suggestions after watching the dragon dance performance prior to the art activity.

- When the dragon is complete, elicit ideas from the children in relation to carrying out the dance together. It may be helpful to play the music to allow the children to experiment with movements to the music. Children could stand behind one another in a line to make a train without holding the dragon they created. Encourage the children to follow and copy the actions of the leader. Encourage the leaders to move along different pathways to the speed of the music. The facilitator may need to discuss fair procedures in relation to alternating leaders and turn taking different roles.
- After the dance, the facilitator may wish to "interview" the children on their experiences of participating in the dragon dance.

Conclusion:

At this point, the facilitator may want to revisit the essential questions to determine whether the children have understood the main ideas of the lesson:

- How is Chinese New Year celebrated?
- What customs followed by Li are similar/different to customs celebrated in your home?
- For those children who do not celebrate Chinese New Year, how are some traditions of *Li's Chinese New Year* similar/different to holidays they celebrate in the winter? What traditions do they have around meal times, gift giving, and celebrations?

As a concluding activity, invite the children to discuss these questions with the whole group, in smaller groups, in pairs, or as a written reflection. An activity such as "Two Stars and a Wish" may be a nice conclusion to the lesson. In pairs, children tell their partner two things they learned and one thing they would like to learn about Chinese New Year.

Assessment:

Facilitator Observation: Children's engagement and interaction with the lesson, engagement in discussions, and engagement with facilitator designed tasks.

Facilitator Questioning: Higher and lower order questioning (i.e., literal, inferential, and evaluative questions).

Facilitator Designed Tasks: Making predictions, vocabulary games, reading fluency activities, dragon art activity, dragon dance movement.

Self-Assessment: "Two Stars and a Wish"

Accommodations/Differentiation:

Differential Modes of Representation:

Photos, pictures, flashcards, video of dragon dance, etc.

Differential Questioning:

Use of higher and lower order questioning (i.e., literal, inferential, and evaluative questions).

Differential Product/Response:

Written responses, oral responses, art responses, movement/dance response.

In a classroom setting, it may be helpful for the English language learners (ELLs) to take the dual language book home either before or after the lesson. The ELL student may read the book at home in the language spoken by his/her family. This will increase the child's confidence when talking about the book in school. If possible, ask the child's parent/guardian to read and record the book in the language that he/she speaks at home. The recording could then be played in the classroom, enabling children to hear other languages spoken by their peers at home.

Extension Activities:

Mask Making (Visual Arts):

Ask the children to briefly retell the story of "The Great Race." Elicit from the children the connection this story has to Chinese New Year. Inform the children that they will create a mask of one of the 12 zodiac animals. The facilitator may wish to follow the guidelines for mask making outlined in the book *Li's Chinese New Year*. It may also be helpful to show examples or pictures of completed masks to help the children to visualize possible creations they can make. Draw children's attention to various features of the 12 different animals (e.g., ears, whiskers, teeth). Ask the children to engage in a Think/Pair/Share activity to discuss possible ideas for their masks with a partner. This will further help children to generate ideas. Following the "Mask Making" instructions from *Li's Chinese New Year*, it may be necessary for the facilitator to demonstrate each step to the children prior to the children carrying out the activity independently. While the children construct their masks, the facilitator may circulate around the room, offering assistance, providing descriptive feedback, and making suggestions to the children. When the children have finished making their masks, ask the children to present their masks to the group. Encourage the children to explain why they chose the particular animals and to describe the colors and patterns they used.

Interview with the Character Li (English – Oral Language):

A piece of clothing (e.g., hat or scarf) will be needed for this activity in order to signify that a child will assume the role of Li from the story.

Preparation for Interview with Character: Ask the children to consider what they would ask Li about his experience of celebrating Chinese New Year if they could meet the character from the story. A Think/Pair/Share activity may be helpful here to help the children formulate questions to ask the character. After the children have shared their questions with the whole group, ask a child to volunteer to assume the role of Li. Inform the children that when the volunteer is wearing the piece of clothing (i.e., hat or scarf), they will assume the role of Li.

Interview with Li: Wearing the piece of clothing, encourage the children to ask some questions about Li's celebration of Chinese New Year. At the end of this activity, the volunteer will remove the piece of clothing used to signify that he/she has returned from the role of Li.

Out of Role Discussion: Ask the children to identify customs and traditions practiced during Chinese New Year. For those students who do not celebrate Chinese New Year, how are some traditions of *Li's Chinese New Year* similar/different to holidays they celebrate in the winter? What traditions do they have around meal times, gift giving, and celebrations?

Project Work on China (Geography):

Develop the children's map reading skills by locating China on a map. Using a large poster/chart, a digital map, or an atlas, ask the children questions to encourage them to examine the physical features of the country. For example, what continent is China in? What countries border China? Is China a landlocked country? What sea borders China? Ask the children to name and locate main cities, rivers and mountains in China.

Additionally, children could conduct independent research on China. Areas of focus for this project work may include:

- *General Information:* Population, capital city, government, language(s), predominant religion, currency, national symbol.
- *Map of China:* Indicate physical features such as capital city, bordering countries, bordering seas, islands, mountain ranges, rivers, and lakes. Note interesting facts about the country's geography (e.g., longest river, highest mountain, largest island).
- *Flag of China:* Picture/sketch of the flag and information about the flag.
- *Language & Culture:* Identify the language(s) spoken in the country with examples of every day phrases. Identify some of the country's art and culture, customs and traditions, traditional dances, and sports.

- **Traditional Food:** Identify examples of traditional dishes, briefly explaining the ingredients.
- **Attractions:** Identify interesting places to visit, tourist attractions, briefly describe the places.
- **Interesting Facts:** Create a "Did you know?" page with some interesting facts learned about the country (e.g., identify a famous person who was born in China).
- **Craft:** Make a craft/item to represent something from the country's culture. For example, make a traditional dish or construct a famous landmark.
- **Similarities and Differences:** Children identify similarities and differences between China and where they live or their countries of birth.

Concept of Number – The Story of 12 (Mathematics - Kindergarten/1st Grade):

The context of "The Great Race" may be used to develop children's number sense. As a warm up activity, ask the children to count to 12 (while performing a kinesthetic action such as jumping or hopping). Next, encourage the children to create sets of 12 by counting. Ask the children to close their eyes and listen to the number of marbles being dropped into a glass jar. For example, the facilitator may choose to drop 8 marbles into the jar, and ask the children to use their fingers to show how many marbles were dropped into the jar. Next, ask the children how many more marbles need to be dropped into the jar to have a total of 12 marbles in the jar. Extending this activity: Ask the children to place cubes on a set placemat to show how many marbles have been placed into the jar (instead of using their fingers). Next, the children must figure out how many more cubes are needed to make 12. Children may then use numerical cards to create an addition sentence.

Vocabulary Flashcards for *Li's Chinese New Year*:

China	Chinese New Year	Chinese zodiac
cobra	Nian	parade
banners	lanterns	dumpling
Kung Hei Fat Choi	Emperor's feast	lucky coin
New Year's celebration	Kalends	new beginnings
lucky sign	dragon dancers	ox
cheating	good luck	bad luck
cunning	charming	graceful
elegant	colorful	mask
shiny	fireworks	celebrate
assembly	coin	packet
even number	fireworks display	New Year's Eve

Theme 3:
Holidays and Festivals

Topic B:
Ramadan -
Samira's Eid

Goal: Provide children with opportunities to learn about and appreciate a range of holidays and festivals celebrated around the world.

Book Used in Lesson: *Samira's Eid*
Written by Nasreen Aktar. Illustrated by Enebor Attard.
Available in English with: Arabic, Bengali, Farsi, French, Kurdish, Panjabi, Somali, Turkish, and Urdu.

Snapshot of Lesson:

- Children make **predictions** about the story based on observations.

- A parcel addressed to the group containing key vocabulary words from the story of *Samira's Eid* arrives. Children **explore key vocabulary** from the story.

- Children listen to a **reading of the story** of *Samira's Eid*

- Children **respond to the text** by answering literal, inferential, and evaluative questions.

- In pairs or small groups, children **retell the story** of *Samira's Eid*, noting Muslim practices during Ramadan.

- Children **respond to the text** by asking Samira or Hassan questions about Ramadan or a key moment in the book (Character Hot Seating).

- Independently, **children create an Eid card**, writing Eid greetings in different languages to Muslims across the world.

Background Information for Facilitator

Ramadan:

Followers of Islam (Muslims), adhere to the *Five Pillars of Islam*. The five pillars are guiding principles for Muslims in their daily lives. The Five Pillars "help strengthen a Muslim's faith, show their obedience" to Allah. The five pillars are:

1. Shahada (Faith)
2. Salah (Prayer)
3. Sawm (Fasting)
4. Zakat (Charity)
5. Hajj (Pilgrimage)

Sawm (fasting) takes place during Ramadan, the ninth month of the Islamic calendar (lunar calendar). During Ramadan, Muslims are expected to begin fasting when they are old enough. For 29 to 40 days, Muslims fast during daylight hours. Fasting requires refraining from all food and drink. Muslims also limit other activities based on cultural beliefs. Muslims eat a meal before sunrise (*Suhur*) and after sunset (*Iftar*). Ramadan concludes with a festival called *Eid ul-Fitr*. Ramadan marks the month when the Qur'an was first revealed. For Muslims, Ramadan is also the time during the Islamic calendar when the gates to heaven are open and the gates to hell are shut.

Sources:

- BBC. (2009). *The five pillars of Islam*. Retrieved from http://www.bbc.co.uk/religion/religions/islam/practices/fivepillars.shtml
- History.com. (2010). *Ramadan*. Retrieved from http://www.history.com/topics/holidays/ramadan
- ISLAMICHistory. (2012). *Ramadan and eid-ul-fitr*. Retrieved from http://islamichistory.org/ramadan-and-eid-ul-fitr/

Lesson Plan: *Samira's Eid*

Grade Level: 3-5 (Note: The activities in this lesson plan can be tailored to suit the needs of the specific group that is being taught, at the discretion of the facilitator.)

Time Frame: 2 x (45 minute - 1 hour) sessions.

Objectives:

Knowledge:

- Learn new vocabulary based on the topic of Ramadan.
- Learn about Muslim practices during Ramadan.

Skills:

- Make predictions based on observations of illustrations.
- Use language to explain and describe.
- Use language to answer and formulate questions.
- Design and make an Eid card.
- Write Eid greetings in different languages from around the world.

Attitudes:

- Appreciate Muslim practices during Ramadan.
- Appreciate the importance of Ramadan to Muslims.

- Value and respect diversity and lifestyles of others.
- Enjoy listening to the story being read in English and in the other language of the dual language book if possible. The story could be read in a second language with the help of a bilingual parent, child, or teacher, or using the PENpal Audio Recorder Pen.
- Appreciate different languages and scripts from around the world.

Essential Questions:

- What do Muslims do during Ramadan?
- Why is Ramadan important to Muslims?
- What customs followed by Samira and Hassan are similar/different to customs celebrated in your home?
- For children who do not participate in Ramadan, how are some traditions of Ramadan similar/different to customs celebrated in their homes? What traditions do they have around fasting?

Materials and Resources:

- *Samira's Eid* by Nasreen Aktar.
- Flashcards of key vocabulary words.
- Parcel addressed to the group containing flashcards with vocabulary words (optional).
- Scarf for Facilitator in Role/Character Hot Seating activity.
- Paper, card, coloring materials, and templates with Eid greetings in languages from countries around the world to make Eid cards (Guidelines included in the book *Samira's Eid*).
- PENpal Audio Recorder Pen (optional).

Linkage and Integration Across Subject Areas:

Language Arts: Vocabulary development, reading, using language to explain and describe, using language to formulate and answer questions, and writing Eid greetings in different languages from around the world (Guidelines included in the book *Samira's Eid*).

Art: Design an Eid card.

Drama: Facilitator in Role/Character Hot Seating (as Samira or Hassan).

Vocabulary to be Developed in Lesson:

Key Vocabulary		Story Specific Vocabulary
• breakfast	• groaned	• Eid
• lunch time	• announced	• Ramadan
• hungry	• new moon	• Muslim
• radio	• dashing	• samosa
• whispered	• gazed	• fasting
• prayed	• dishes	• Zahat
• teacher	• gasped	• Mecca
• present	• feast	• Islam
• book	• empty	• Shalwar-Kameez
• cards	• ordinary	• mosque
• aunts	• sunrise	• imam
• uncles	• pale	
• friends	• post (mail)	
• neighbors		

Expressions

Hassan couldn't stop himself from complaining.

Samira and Hassan could hardly believe their eyes.

Eid Mubarak (Greeting).

Samira had curled up on the sofa next to Nani.

Procedure:

Introduction:

1. Begin the lesson by presenting the cover of the book. Draw the children's attention to the mosque on the cover in the book. Ask the children to identify some physical characteristics of the mosque (e.g., dome-shaped roof, tall slender tower called a minaret, decorative patterns on the windows).

2. Elicit from the children what community attends a mosque and why that community goes there; that is, Muslims primarily go to the mosque to pray and celebrate religious events such as Ramadan.

3. Ask the children who they think the people standing outside the mosque on the cover of the book are? What are they doing? Why do you think they are outside the mosque? With these observations in mind, ask the children to predict what they think the story will be about.

Vocabulary Development:

4. Inform the children that a parcel addressed to the group arrived containing important words that they will need to learn before reading the story.

5. Using the list of words tabulated above or any additional words, elicit known vocabulary (key vocabulary/story specific vocabulary) on the topic of Ramadan. This activity can be supported by the use of flashcards and/or pictures.

6. Present new vocabulary (key vocabulary /story specific vocabulary) to the children. Using flashcards and/or pictures, invite the children to say/read each word. Ask the children if they know the meanings of the words and encourage them to provide explanations of the words if possible. The facilitator may need to elaborate or provide additional explanations of some words and say the words in sentences so the students can hear the words in context. The facilitator may ask the children to create their own sentences containing the words, encouraging the children to make personal connections with the words. If there are bilingual children in the group, it may be possible to ask them to say the words in their language(s).

Reading:

7. Read the book *Samira's Eid* with the children. The facilitator may choose to read the book aloud to the children, engage in choral reading (facilitator and children read the story together in unison), or see-saw reading (facilitator reads one sentence, children read the following sentence and continue alternating reading after each sentence). It is important to read with appropriate tone, pace, inflection, and expression to engage the children as much as possible. If there are children who speak the language of the dual language book, here would be a nice opportunity to ask them to read/translate a section of the story if they would like. Moreover, if the facilitator has a PENpal Audio Recorder, the children could listen to a reading of the story in English or the other language of the dual language book.

8. Throughout the story, explicitly draw children's attention to the illustrations to promote comprehension of the text.

9. Encourage children to make connections (orally, using mime, in writing). Connections may be *text-to-self* (what does the child notice from the book in relation to his/her own lived experiences), *text-to-text* (what does the child notice from one book/story to another book/story), or *text-to-wider-world* (what does the child notice from the book in relation to real world historical or current contexts).

Discussion to Encourage Reflection and Response:

10. Facilitate discussion with the group of children using literal, inferential, and evaluative questions. The facilitator may wish to select questions from the following list:

Literal Questions:

(Readers use information directly from the text to answer this type of question.)

   i. *When were Samira and Hassan making cards?*
   ii. *Why did Hassan dash to the window the night before Eid?*
   iii. *What was lying on Samira's bed?*
   iv. *Who did everyone in the mosque listen to?*
   v. *What gift did Nani give to Samira and Hassan?*

Inferential Questions:

(Reader must use the information in the text to deduce the answer.)

   i. *Why does Samira tell Hassan to "think about all the people who are fasting just like us"?*
   ii. *Why does Mum tell Hassan to "think of all the people who can only have one meal a day"?*
   iii. *Were the children happy to see their teacher, Mrs. Qadir, outside the mosque? Why?*
   iv. *Why was there an empty chair at the table? Who do you think it was for?*

Evaluative Questions:

(Reader uses his/her own knowledge to explore answers to this type of question.)

   i. *How do you think Hassan felt about fasting for Ramadan?*
   ii. *How do you think Samira and Hassan felt when they told their father that they fasted just like he did?*
   iii. *How do you think Samira felt when no card from Nani arrived in the post?*
   iv. *What do you think the book that Nani gave to Samira and Hassan is about?*

Word Identification/Fluency Development:

11. ***Revisit the Story and Identify Key Vocabulary Words:*** Display key vocabulary words from the story. Reread a section from the story and ask the children to raise their hands when they hear or see one of the key vocabulary words.

12. **Retell the Story:** Present key words from the story listed in order as they appear in the story. Using the words, children retell the story in small groups or pairs. The facilitator may ask the children to retell the story orally or in writing. The facilitator may present sentences with key words for this activity to provide the children with additional support. The children could also retell the story using illustrations, mime or still images.

Independent Work/Group Work Activity

13. **Facilitator in Role & Hot Seating Drama Activity:**
   - A piece of clothing (e.g., hat or scarf) will be needed for this activity in order to signify that the facilitator will assume the role of Hassan from the story.
   - **Preparation for Facilitator in Role:** Ask the children to consider what they would ask Hassan if they could meet the characters from the story. A Think/Pair/Share activity may be useful here to help the children formulate questions to ask the characters.
   - **Facilitator in Role:** After the children have shared their questions with the whole group, inform the children that when the facilitator is wearing the piece of clothing (i.e., hat or scarf), they will assume the role of Hassan.
   - **Character Hot Seating:** Wearing the piece of clothing, thank the children for showing such interest in learning about his experience during Ramadan. Next, invite the children to ask some questions about the customs Hassan and his family follow during Ramadan. At the end of this activity, the facilitator will take off the piece of clothing used to signify that he/she has returned from the role of Hassan.

14. **Independent Art Activity:**
   - Children design and create an Eid card, writing wishes to Muslims who are participating in Ramadan in different languages from around the world.
   - Guidelines, design templates, and greetings in different languages are included in the book *Samira's Eid* to help facilitate this activity.

Conclusion:

At this point, the facilitator may wish to revisit essential questions to determine whether the children have understood the main ideas of the lesson:

   - *What do Muslims do during Ramadan?*
   - *Why is Ramadan important to Muslims?*
   - *What customs followed by Samira and Hassan are similar/different to customs celebrated in your home?*
   - *For children who do not participate in Ramadan, how are some traditions of Ramadan similar/different to customs celebrated in their homes? What traditions do they have around fasting?*

As a concluding activity, invite the children to discuss these questions with the whole group, in smaller groups, in pairs, or as a written reflection. An activity such as "Two Stars and a Wish" may be a nice conclusion to the lesson. In pairs, children identify two things they have learned and one thing they would like to learn about Ramadan.

Assessment:

Facilitator Observation: Children's engagement and interaction with the lesson, engagement in discussions, and engagement with facilitator designed tasks.

Facilitator Questioning: Higher and lower order questioning (i.e., literal, inferential, and evaluative questions).

Facilitator Designed Tasks: Making predictions, vocabulary games, reading fluency activities, drama activity (hot-seating), card making activity.

Self-Assessment: "Two Stars and a Wish"

Accommodations/Differentiation:

Differential Modes of Representation:

Photos, pictures, flashcards, etc.

Differential Questioning:

Use of higher and lower order questioning (i.e., literal, inferential and evaluative questions).

Differential Product/Response:

Written responses, oral responses, drama responses, art responses.

In a classroom setting, it may be helpful for the English language learners (ELLs) to take the dual language book home either before or after the lesson. The ELL student may read the book at home in the language spoken by his/her family. This will increase the child's confidence when talking about the book in school. If possible, ask the child's parent/guardian to read and record the book in the language that he/she speaks at home. The recording could then be played in the classroom, enabling children to hear other languages spoken by their peers at home.

Extension Activities:

Diary Entry (English – Independent Writing):

The facilitator may wish to extend children's engagement with *Samira's Eid* through descriptive writing exercises. Children could write a diary entry as a character in the story. The children could focus on a key moment from the story such as writing Eid cards or receiving the gift from Nani.

Writing a Blurb (English – Shared Writing):

An additional writing exercise may include writing a blurb suitable for the book *Samira's Eid*. Alternatively, the children could write a blurb suitable for the book that Samira and Hassan received as a gift from Nani. It is important to display examples of book jackets and blurbs. Ask the children to identify the features of a blurb (e.g., writing to encourage others to read the book, not writing the whole story or giving away the ending). As writing a blurb may be challenging for some students, this activity could be carried out as a shared writing exercise, whereby the facilitator acts as scribe and writes the children's ideas. After this support from the facilitator, the children may be able to write blurbs in pairs or independently.

Extending the Story of *Samira's Eid* (English - Oral Language):

Engage in a group discussion about the book that Samira and Hassan received as a gift from Nani. Elicit from the children their thoughts about what the content of the book could be. In pairs or small groups, children could work together to compose a story in their own words. Flashcards with key vocabulary words or pictures from the story could be displayed to support children with this task. There are pictures from the story of *Samira's Eid* included in the back of the book *Samira's Eid* that may be used for this activity. Additionally, children may wish to create "still images" or "freeze frames" to illustrate key moments from their stories. This involves the children working together to create images using their bodies. Each group can share its version of the story with the whole group of children.

2D Shapes/Tessellation (Mathematics/Visual Art): Looking at and responding to tessellations in Islamic Art can be integrated with mathematics. Pattern blocks or online tools may be used to provide children with opportunities to tessellate 2D shapes. Children may create their own tessellation artworks by constructing a template. Before the children carry out the art activity independently, it will be necessary for the facilitator to demonstrate the steps tabulated below to the children.

Step	Visual Example
Step 1 Sketch a simple line design on one side of a square-shaped piece of card. Label this line **A** and label the opposite side of the card **A** Next, draw another simple line design, Label the line **B** and label the opposite side of the square **B** also	
Step 2 Cut along, the line A and B. There will now be three pieces of card. Attach piece A and piece B to part A and B of the shape (See picture).	
Step 3 Place the shape on a sheet of paper and trace along the outline of the shape, Next, align the shape with the outline drawn and trace the outline of the shape once again. Continue tracing the tessellation onto the paper.	

Finally, children may decorate the shape using colored pencils, markers, or crayons. Moreover, encourage the children to individualize their tessellation squares by drawing repeated designs on each shape. Facilitate a whole group discussion, enabling children to look and respond to one another's art pieces. Encourage the children to identify and describe the tessellating shapes.

Project Work on the Middle East (Geography):

A map of the Middle East is included in the book *Samira's Eid*. The map indicates Islamic Countries (countries and regions where Muslims make up the majority). Develop the children's map reading skills by locating different countries on the map.

The facilitator may wish to focus on a particular country or countries by using a large poster/chart, a digital map, or an atlas. Ask the children questions to encourage them to examine the physical features of the country. For example, what continent is the country Algeria in? What countries border Algeria? Is Algeria a landlocked country? What sea borders Algeria? Ask the children to name and locate main cities, rivers and mountains in Algeria.

Additionally, children could conduct independent research on a country in the Middle East such as Algeria. Areas of focus for this project work may include:

- **General Information:** Population, capital city, government, language(s), predominant religion, currency, national symbol.
- **Map of Algeria:** Indicate physical features such as capital city, bordering seas, islands, mountain ranges, rivers, and lakes. Note interesting facts about the country's geography (e.g., longest river, highest mountain, largest island).
- **Flag of Algeria:** Picture/sketch of the flag and information about the flag.
- **Language & Culture:** Identify the language(s) spoken in the country with examples of every day phrases. Identify some of the country's art and culture, customs and traditions, traditional dances and sports.
- **Traditional Food:** Identify examples of traditional dishes, briefly explaining the ingredients.
- **Attractions:** Identify interesting places to visit, tourist attractions, briefly describe the places.
- **Interesting Facts:** Create a "Did you know?" page with some interesting facts learned about the country (e.g., identify a famous person who was born in Algeria).
- **Craft:** Make a craft/item to represent something from the country's culture. For example, make a traditional dish or construct a famous landmark.
- **Similarities and Differences:** Children identify similarities and differences between Algeria and where they live or their countries of birth.

Vocabulary Flashcards for *Samira's Eid*:

Eid	Ramadan	Muslim
samosa	fasting	zahat
Mecca	Islam	Shalwar-kameez
mosque	imam	groaned
announced	new moon	dashing
gazed	dishes	feast
empty	ordinary	sunrise
pale	post	hungry
radio	whispered	prayed
present	book	cards
aunts	uncles	neighbors
friends	teacher	breakfast

Theme 3:
Holidays and Festivals

Topic C:
Diwali –
Deepak's Diwali

Goal: Provide children with opportunities to learn about and appreciate a range of holidays and festivals celebrated around the world.

Book Used in Lesson: *Deepak's Diwali*
Written by Divya Karwal. Illustrated by Doreen Lang.
Available in English with: Arabic, Bengali, French, Gujarati, Hindi, Malayalam, Nepali, Panjabi, Polish, Tamil, and Urdu.

Prior to the lesson:

- It is recommended to introduce to the story of Rama and Sita to the children prior to reading *Deepak's Diwali*.

- Information on this story can be found at the end of the book *Deepak's Diwali* using the PENpal Audio Recorder Pen.

- The following websites also have information on the story of Rama and Sita (different versions of the story):
  - http://www.bbc.co.uk/learning/schoolradio/subjects/collectiveworship/collectiveworship_stories/festivals/diwali
  - https://www.youtube.com/watch?v=uad2pS_T80I
  - https://www.youtube.com/watch?v=mkbxhUeqBTo

Snapshot of Lesson:

- Children use their **prior knowledge** of the story of Rama and Sita and the illustrations on the cover of the book to **predict** the story *Deepak's Diwali*.

- Children **explore key vocabulary** from the story.

- Children listen to a **reading of the story** of *Deepak's Diwali*.

- Children **respond to the text** by answering literal, inferential, and evaluative questions.

- In pairs or small groups, children **retell the story** of *Deepak's Diwali*.

- In small groups, children **make shadow puppets** and create a performance to tell the story of Rama and Sita.

Background Information for Facilitator

Diwali:

Diwali is a five-day festival celebrated by followers of Hinduism and is commonly known as the festival of lights. Historical perspectives underpinning the festival vary in different parts of India. Although the festival celebrates Rama's return to Ayodhya, some Hindus worship other deities at Diwali also. Some Hindus worship the goddess of strength, Kali. Others worship Lord Ganesha, the elephant-headed god of wisdom. In the story of *Deepak's Diwali*, Deepak's family remembers Lakshmi, the goddess of wealth and luck.

Hindus decorate homes, shops, and streets with rows of decorative candles, lights, and diyas (oil lamps). The word "Diwali" means "row of lights (or lamps)". The lights welcome the goddess Lakshmi into people's homes, bringing in goodness and hope, driving away evil. On festival days, Hindus often rub their hair with sweet smelling herbs and oils. Women and girls often decorate their hands with henna (mehndi). Most Hindu families have a shrine so that the family can pray together in front of pictures of their gods and offer them gifts of fruit, rice, sweets, and spices.

Sources:

- Authors of National Geographic KiDS. (2008). *Diwali: Festival of lights*. Retrieved from National Geographic KiDS https://kids.nationalgeographic.com/explore/diwali/
- BBC. (2009). *BBC Religion: Hinduism*. Retrieved from BBC http://www.bbc.co.uk/religion/religions/hinduism/
- Encyclopaedia, B. I. (2010). *2010 britannica student encyclopedia*, 4 (D & E), p.58.
- Encyclopaedia, B. I. (2010). *2010 britannica student encyclopedia*, 6 (H & I), p.56.
- PENpal Audio Recorder Pen audio recording in Karwal, D., & Lang, D. (2009). *Deepak's Diwali*. London, UK: Mantra Lingua Ltd.
- Society for the Confluence of Festivals in India. (2017). *Diwali*. Retrieved from http://www.diwalifestival.org/

Lesson Plan: *Deepak's Diwali*

Grade Level: 3-5 (Note: The activities in this lesson plan can be tailored to suit the needs of the specific group that is being taught, at the discretion of the facilitator.)

Time Frame: 2 x (45 minute - 1 hour) sessions.

Objectives:

Knowledge:

- Learn new vocabulary based on the topic of Diwali.
- Learn about Hindu practices during Diwali.

Skills:

- Retell the story of Rama and Sita.
- Make predictions based on observations of illustrations.
- Use language to explain and describe.
- Design and make shadow puppets to tell the story of Rama and Sita.
- Create a performance to tell the story of Rama and Sita.

Attitudes:

- Appreciate Hindu practices during Diwali.
- Appreciate the importance of Diwali to Hindus.
- Value and respect diversity and lifestyles of others.
- Enjoy listening to the story being read in English and in the other language of the dual language book if possible. The story could be read in a second language with the help of a bilingual parent, child, or teacher, or using the PENpal Audio Recorder Pen.
- Appreciate different languages and scripts from around the world.

Essential Questions:

- What is the connection between the story of Diwali and the story of Rama and Sita?
- How is Diwali celebrated by Deepak similar/different to customs celebrated in your home?
- For those children who do not celebrate Diwali, how are some traditions of Diwali similar/different to holidays they celebrate? What traditions do they have around meal times, prayer, gift giving?

Materials and Resources:

- *Deepak's Diwali* by Divya Karwal.
- Flashcards with pictures of key vocabulary words.
- Parcel addressed to the group containing flashcards with vocabulary words (optional).
- Construction paper, scissors, craft sticks, tape (shadow puppets).

- Large box, sheet of white tissue paper, torch/lamp (mini theater for shadow puppet performance).
- PENpal Audio Recorder Pen (optional).

Linkage and Integration across subject areas:

Language Arts: Vocabulary development, reading, using language to explain and describe, using language to formulate and answer questions.

Art: Design and make shadow puppets.

Drama: Create a performance to tell the story of *Rama and Sita* using shadow puppets.

Vocabulary to be Developed in Lesson:

Key Vocabulary		Story specific vocabulary
• stole • breakfast • whispered • late • costume • pirate • proud,proudly • stepped • envelopes • drops of water • forehead • doorbell • windowsill • losing • scared • garden • fighting; attacking • battle • warrior	• hushed voice • sparklers • fairy lights • chasing • borrow • India • wink • pray • powder • blessing • peace • gobbled • midnight • hugged • diamonds • crackling;crackled; fizzing; sputtered • revenge • fiercely • rescued • celebration • lump of clay • twirled	• diwali • Deepak (clay lamps/ source of light) • demon king • rangoli patterns • samosas • ladoos (yellow sweet balls) • offer to the gods • kurta-paijama • oil lamps • bad spirits • Tika • aarti • chickpea curry • Paneer • fried puree bread • Halwa pudding • clay lamps • burfis • Robin Hood

Expressions

Deepak hid under the covers.

Tim tried to keep a straight face.

The delicious smells coming from the kitchen made Deepak's mouth water.

Deepak couldn't resist anymore and gobbled down one of the delicious sweets.

Names and Pronunciations of Characters in *Deepak's Diwali*

Deepak, Dadi (da/di: Hindi word for paternal grandmother), Dad, Mum, Tim (Deepak's best friend), Nani (naa/ny : maternal grandmother), Nana (naa/na: maternal grandfather), Aunty, Uncle, cousin Tara.

Characters from Hindu Mythology mentioned in *Deepak's Diwali*: Ravana (demon king), Rama, Sita (Rama's wife), Hanuman (monkey warrior), Lakshman (Rama's brother), Lakshmi (goddess).

Procedure:

Introduction:

1. Begin lesson by presenting the sequence of pictures illustrating the story of Rama and Sita at end of the book *Deepak's Diwali*.

2. Ask the children to retell the story of Rama and Sita (Alternatively, the group could listen to the story of Rama and Sita at the end of the story book *Deepak's Diwali* using the PENpal Audio Recorder Pen).

3. Ask the children why people lined the path with rows of candles as Rama and Sita made their way home. (The people celebrated their return home).

4. Ask the children to identify the characters illustrated on the cover of the book (Rama, Sita, Ravana, Haunman).

5. Draw children's attention to the boy (Deepak) who is depicted on the cover of the book. What is he holding?

6. Ask the children to predict what they think the story will be about based on their observations of the illustrations on the cover of the book.

Vocabulary Development:

7. Inform the children that a parcel addressed to the group arrived containing important words that they will need to learn before reading the story.

8. Using the list of words tabulated above or any additional words, elicit known vocabulary (key vocabulary/story specific vocabulary) on the topic of Diwali. This activity can be supported by the use of flashcards and/or pictures.

9. Present new vocabulary (key vocabulary /story specific vocabulary) to the children. Using flashcards and/or pictures, invite the children to say/read each word. Ask the children if they know the meanings of the words and encourage them to provide explanations of the words if possible. The facilitator may need to elaborate or provide additional explanations of some words and say the words in sentences so the students can hear the words in context. The facilitator may ask the children to create their own sentences containing the words, encouraging the children to make personal connections with the words. If there are bilingual children in the group, it may be possible to ask them to say the words in their language(s).

Reading:

10. Read the book *Deepak's Diwali* with the children. The facilitator may choose to read the book aloud to the children, engage in choral reading (facilitator and children read the story together in unison), or see-saw reading (facilitator reads one sentence, children read the following sentence and continue alternating reading after each sentence). It is important to read with appropriate tone, pace, inflection, and expression to engage the children as much as possible. If there are children who speak the language of the dual language book, here would be a nice opportunity to ask them to read/translate a section of the story if they would like. Moreover, if the facilitator has a PENpal Audio Recorder Pen, the children could listen to a reading of the story in English or the other language of the dual language book.

11. Throughout the story, explicitly draw children's attention to the illustrations to promote comprehension of the text.

12. Encourage children to make connections (orally, using mime, in writing). Connections may be *text-to-self* (what does the child notice from the book in relation to his/her own lived experiences), *text-to-text* (what does the child notice from one book/story to another book/story), or *text-to-wider-world* (what does the child notice from the book in relation to real world historical or current contexts).

Discussion to Encourage Reflection and Response:

13. Facilitate discussion with the group of children using literal, inferential, and evaluative questions. The facilitator may wish to select questions from the following list:

Literal Questions:

(Readers use information directly from the text to answer this type of question.)

   i.   *What story did Dadi tell Deepak?*
   ii.   *What did Ravana look like?*
   iii. *What was Deepak's favorite part of Diwali?*
   iv.   *Who did Deepak think was coming after him?*
   v.   *What country were the Diwali cards sent from?*
   vi.   *Where did they place the oil lamps?*
   vii. *What does Deepak's name mean?*

Inferential Questions:

(Reader must use the information in the text to deduce the answer.)

   i.   *Why do you think Deepak hid under the covers when Dadi told him the story?*
   ii.   *Why does Deepak's mother tell him to eat a sandwich instead of some ladoos?*
   iii. *Why do you think the oil lamps kept blowing out?*

Evaluative Questions:

(Reader uses his/her own knowledge to explore answers to this type of question.)

   i.   *What do you think Tim was thinking when Deepak told him that Ravana, the demon king, was after him?*
   ii.   *Do you think Deepak, Tim, and Tara are enjoying themselves when they are pretending to help Hanuman fight Ravana? Why/Why not?*
   iii. *Why do you think Tim changed his mind about dressing up as Robin Hood for the school party?*

Word Identification/Fluency Development:

14. ***Revisit the Story and Identify Key Vocabulary Words***: Display key vocabulary words from the story. Reread a section from the story and ask the children to raise their hands when they hear or see one of the key vocabulary words.

15. ***Retell the Story (in pairs or small groups):*** Present key words from the story listed in order as they appear in the story. Using the words, children retell the story in small groups or pairs. The facilitator may ask the children to retell the story orally or in writing. The facilitator may present sentences with key words for this activity to provide the children with additional support. The children could also retell the story using illustrations, mime, or still images.

Independent Work/Group Work Activity:

16. ***Making Shadow Puppets & Perform the Story of Rama and Sita***
    - Inform the children that they will work together in groups to make shadow puppets and to create a performance of the story of Rama and Sita.
    - Before making the puppets, ask the children to retell the story of Rama and Sita in their own words. Alternatively, the facilitator may play an audio recording of the story for the children to listen to using the PENpal Audio Recorder Pen. Information on this story can be found at the end of the book.
    - Elicit from the children what puppets will need to be made (i.e., Rama, Sita, Ravana, Hanuman).
    - Model how to create a shadow puppet: First, draw an outline of the character (for younger children a pre-drawn template of the character may be helpful). Next, cut around the outline. Using tape, attach a craft stick to the back of the character puppet.
    - After the shadow puppets are made, allow the children to practice their performances. The facilitator may wish to display flashcards of key vocabulary words from the story in order to support the groups when creating their stories. After the children have practiced their performances, each group may perform the story.
    - Shadow Puppet Performance: A simple shadow puppet theater may be constructed by cutting out the bottom of a cardboard box (this is the front of the theater). Then attach a sheet of white tissue paper over the part of the box that was cut. Finally, place a lamp/torch behind the box, shining onto the sheet of white tissue paper.

Conclusion:

At this point, the facilitator may want to revisit essential questions to determine whether the children have understood the main ideas of the lesson:

- *What is the connection between the story of Diwali and the story of Rama and Sita?*
- *How is Diwali celebrated by Deepak similar/different to customs celebrated in your home?*
- *For those children who do not celebrate Diwali, how are some traditions of Diwali similar/different to holidays they celebrate? What traditions do they have around meal times, prayer, gift giving?*

As a concluding activity, invite the children to discuss these questions with the whole group, in smaller groups, in pairs, or as a written reflection. An activity such as "Two Stars and a Wish" may be a nice conclusion to the lesson. In pairs, children identify two things that they learned and one thing they would like to learn about Diwali.

Assessment:

Facilitator Observation: Children's engagement and interaction with the lesson, engagement in discussions, and engagement with facilitator designed tasks.

Facilitator Questioning: Higher and lower order questioning (i.e., literal, inferential, and evaluative questions).

Facilitator Designed Tasks: Making predictions, vocabulary games, reading fluency activities, shadow puppet activity, shadow puppet performance.

Self-Assessment: "Two Stars and a Wish"

Accommodations/Differentiation:

Differential modes of Representation:

Photos, pictures, flashcards, etc.

Differential Questioning:

Use of higher and lower order questioning (i.e., literal, inferential, and evaluative questions).

Differential Product/Response:

Written responses, oral responses, art responses, drama responses.

In a classroom setting, it may be helpful for the English language learners (ELLs) to take the dual language book home either before or after the lesson. The ELL student may read the book at home in the language spoken by his/her family. This will increase the child's confidence when talking about the book in school. If possible, ask the child's parent/guardian to read and record the book in the language that he/she speaks at home. The recording could then be played in the classroom, enabling children to hear other languages spoken by their peers at home.

Extension Activities:

Writing a Postcard (Independent Writing - English):

The facilitator may wish to extend children's engagement with *Deepak's Diwali* through a persuasive writing exercise. Children could write a postcard from Deepak to Nani and

Nana in India. Writing in role as the character Deepak, the child could describe his family's Diwali celebrations to his grandparents.

Symmetry (Mathematics):

Looking at and responding to Rangoli patterns can be integrated with mathematics. The facilitator may wish to follow the guidelines for making Rangoli patterns outlined in the book *Deepak's Diwali*. Present various Rangoli patterns to the children, encouraging them to identify lines of symmetry. Children can copy Rangoli patterns onto grid paper, drawing lines of symmetry. Alternatively, children may create their own Rangoli pattern using grid paper, ensuring the patterns are symmetrical.

Clay Tea Light Candleholders (Visual Arts):

Ask the children where Deepak and his parents placed the oil lamps in the story *Deepak's Diwali*. Why did they put out oil lamps? Present photographs of Diwali oil lamps to the children. Look and respond to various oil lamps in relation to patterns, rhythm, designs, and colors. Inform the children that they will make a candleholder for a tea light candle using clay. The facilitator will need to demonstrate the steps involved in making a candleholder prior to the children carrying out the activity independently. One possibility is to roll a piece of clay into a ball and then make a hollow in the center by pressing a tea light candle down onto the clay. The facilitator may wish to demonstrate simple techniques to decorate the piece also. While the children construct their candleholders, the facilitator may circulate around the room, offering assistance, providing descriptive feedback, and making suggestions to the children. When the children have completed making their candleholders, ask the children to present their finished artworks to the group. Encourage the children to describe the colors and patterns they used.

Project Work on India (Geography):

Develop the children's map reading skills by locating India on a map. Using a large poster/chart, a digital map, or an atlas, ask the children questions to encourage them to examine the physical features of the country. For example, what continent is India in? What countries border India? Is India a landlocked country? What sea borders India? Ask the children to name and locate main cities, rivers, and mountains in India.

Additionally, children could conduct independent research on India. Areas of focus for this project work may include:

- *General Information:* Population, capital city, government, language(s), predominant religion, currency, national symbol.

- **Map of India:** Indicate physical features such as capital city, bordering seas, islands, mountain ranges, rivers, and lakes. Note interesting facts about the country's geography (e.g., longest river, highest mountain, largest island).
- **Flag of India:** Picture/sketch of the flag and information about the flag.
- **Language & Culture:** Identify the language(s) spoken in the country with examples of every day phrases. Identify some of the country's art and culture, customs and traditions, traditional dances, and sports.
- **Traditional Food:** Identify examples of traditional dishes, briefly explaining the ingredients.
- **Attractions:** Identify interesting places to visit, tourist attractions, briefly describe the places.
- **Interesting Facts:** Create a "Did you know?" page with some interesting facts learned about the country (e.g., identify a famous person who was born in India).
- **Craft:** Make a craft/item to represent something from the country's culture. For example, make a traditional dish or construct a famous landmark.
- **Similarities and Differences:** Children identify similarities and differences between India and where they live or their countries of birth.

Vocabulary Flashcards for *Deepak's Diwali*:

Diwali	Deepak	demon king
rangoli patterns	samosas	ladoos
offer to the gods	Kurta-Paijama	oil lamps
bad spirits	tika	aarti
chickpea curry	Paneer	fried puree bread
Halwa pudding	clay lamps	burfis
Robin Hood	hushed voice	sparklers
fairy lights	chasing	guests
borrow	India	wink
pray	powder	blessing
peace	gobbled	midnight
lump of clay	battle	warrior

Theme 3:
Holidays and Festivals

Topic D:
Polish Christmas –
Marek and Alice's Christmas

Goal: Provide children with opportunities to learn about and appreciate a range of holidays and festivals celebrated around the world.

Book Used in Lesson: *Marek and Alice's Christmas*
Written by Jolanta Starek-Corile. Illustrated by Priscilla Lamont.
Available in English with: Albanian, Arabic, Bulgarian, Croatian, Czech, French, Lithuanian, Polish, Portuguese, Romanian, Russian, Spanish, Urdu, and Welsh.

Snapshot of Lesson:

- Children make **predictions** about the story based on observations.

- Children "**travel to Poland**" during the story to observe Christmas traditions in Poland.

- Children prepare for their journey by unpacking a suitcase of **key vocabulary words**.

- Children listen to a **reading of the story** of *Marek and Alice's Christmas*.

- Children **respond to the text** by answering literal, inferential, and evaluative questions.

- In pairs or small groups, children **retell the story** of *Marek and Alice's Christmas*.

- Children **listen and respond** to Christmas Carol *Cicha Noc* (Silent Night in Polish)

- Children **respond to the text** by asking Alice or Marek questions about Christmas in Poland (Facilitator in Role/Character Hot Seating).

Background Information for Facilitator

Christmas in Poland:

Christmas has been celebrated in Poland since the late 10th century when Christianity began in Poland. Many people in Poland follow Christmas customs recognized in other countries as well. The Polish Christmas traditions include:

1. Attending Mass every day (or week) during Advent. Advent is a period of preparation leading up to Christmas. It begins on the fourth Sunday before Christmas Day. Christmas Eve concludes with Midnight Mass.

2. Celebrating Christmas Eve by fasting after breakfast until sighting the first star in the night sky.

3. Sighting the first star marks the beginning of the Christmas Eve meal *Wigilia*.

4. Receiving some gifts on St. Nicolas' Day (December 6th) and some gifts from Star Man (symbolizing the Star of Bethlehem) after Christmas Eve dinner.

5. Christmas Eve meal traditions include:
    *   Serving at least twelve dishes as part of the Christmas Eve meal. This symbolizes the Twelve Apostles.
    *   Setting an extra place at the table for an unexpected guest, symbolizing Mary and Joseph's quest to find shelter.
    *   Not eating meat at the Christmas Eve meal (an old Catholic tradition). Other foods eaten include carp (fish), makowiec (baked poppy seed bread), and kutia (poppy seed and wheat pasta with honey, raisons, almonds, and spices).

Sources Cited:

*   Country Reports. (n.d.). *Poland Christmas Tradition*. Retrieved from http://www.countryreports.org/country/Poland/christmastraditions.htm
*   Cooper, J. (2014). *Christmas in Poland*. Retrieved from https://www.whychristmas.com/cultures/poland.shtml

Lesson Plan: *Marek and Alice's Christmas*

Grade Level: 3-5 (Note: The activities in this lesson plan can be tailored to suit the needs of the specific group that is being taught, at the discretion of the facilitator.)

Time Frame: 2 x (45 minute - 1 hour) sessions.

Objectives:

Knowledge:

*   Learn new vocabulary based on the topic of Christmas.
*   Learn about Christmas traditions in Poland.

Skills:

*   Make predictions based on observations of illustrations.
*   Use language to explain and describe.
*   Use language to answer and formulate questions.
*   Listen and respond to *Cicha Noc* (Silent Night in Polish).

Attitudes:

- Appreciate that people in other countries celebrate Christmas.
- Appreciate the Christmas traditions in Poland.
- Value and respect diversity and lifestyles of others.
- Enjoy listening to the story being read in English and in the other language of the dual language book if possible. The story could be read in a second language with the help of a bilingual parent, child, or teacher, or using the PENpal Audio Recorder Pen.
- Appreciate different languages and scripts around the world.

Essential Questions:

- How is Christmas celebrated in Poland?
- What Christmas customs followed by Marek and Alice are similar/different to customs celebrated in your home?
- For those children who do not celebrate Christmas, how are some traditions of Polish Christmas similar/different to holidays they celebrate in the winter? What traditions do they have around meal times, gift giving, and singing?

Materials and Resources:

- *Marek and Alice's Christmas* by Jolanta Starek-Corile.
- Flashcards of key vocabulary words.
- Suitcase (for vocabulary words activity – optional).
- *Cicha Noc* (Silent Night in Polish): https://www.youtube.com/watch?v=4UUcVWNrAQ8
- Piece of clothing (e.g., hat or scarf) for Facilitator in Role/Character Hot Seating activity.
- PENpal Audio Recorder Pen (optional).

Linkage and Integration across subject areas:

Language Arts: Vocabulary development, reading, using language to explain and describe, using language to formulate and answer questions.

Music: *Cicha Noc* (Silent Night in Polish).

Drama: Role Play (traveling to Poland), Facilitator in Role/Character Hot Seating activity.

Vocabulary to be Developed in Lesson:

Key Vocabulary		Story specific vocabulary
• Christmas • Christmas decorations • Christmas tree • prayer • present • star • sing • supper • chips (fries) • extra plate	• doorbell • hay • Jesus • stable • quad bike • carols • wrapping presents • unpack • welcome	• pine tree • carp (fish) • Star of Bethlehem • blessed bread • recorder (instrument) • Silent Night (Christmas carol) • St. Nicolas' Day • Midnight Mass • offer wishes • greeted • fast (fasting)

Expressions

He beamed with joy.

The more dishes you try, the more rich and plentiful your life will be.

Names and Pronunciations of Characters in *Marek and Alice's Christmas*

Alice, Marek, Mum, Dad, dziadek (grandfather: *jah-Dek*), babcia (grandmother: *bob-cha/bop-cha*), prababcia (great grandmother: *pra-bob-cha/pra-bop-cha*), Uncle Waldek, Olek, and Borys (the family's pet dog).

Procedure:

Introduction:

1. Begin the lesson by presenting the cover of the book to the children and elicit what time of year they think it is in the picture. Ask the children to explain their responses.

2. Ask the children to identify customs and/or traditional items associated with Christmas. Inform the children that Christmas is celebrated all over the world but it is celebrated in different ways. Using clues on the cover of the book, ask the children what country they think the story is set in and to explain their reasoning. The facilitator may need to draw children's attention to Alice's dress and inform the children that this is a traditional Polish dress.

3. Draw children's attention to the star on the cover in the book. Ask the children to predict what they think is the significance of the star to the book. Encourage the children to use their observations to predict the content of the story.

4. Inform the group that they are boarding a plane/train "to travel to Poland" to see how people in another country celebrate Christmas.

Vocabulary Development:

5. Inform the group that they have a suitcase filled with the important words that they will need to learn before their trip.

6. Using the list of words noted above or any additional words, elicit known vocabulary (familiar/less familiar vocabulary) on the topic of Christmas. This activity can be supported by the use of flashcards and/or pictures.

7. Present new vocabulary (key vocabulary /story specific vocabulary) to the children. Using flashcards and/or pictures, invite the children to say/read each word. Ask the children if they know the meanings of the words and encourage them to provide explanations of the words if possible. The facilitator may need to elaborate or provide additional explanations of some words and say the words in sentences so the students can hear the words in context. The facilitator may ask the children to create their own sentences containing the words, encouraging the children to make personal connections with the words. If there are bilingual children in the group, it may be possible to ask them to say the words in their language(s).

Reading:

8. Read the book *Marek and Alice's Christmas* with the children. The facilitator may choose to read the book aloud to the children, engage in choral reading (facilitator and children read the story together in unison), or see-saw reading (facilitator reads one sentence, children read the following sentence and continue alternating reading after each sentence). It is important to read with appropriate tone, pace, inflection, and expression to engage the children as much as possible. If there are children who speak the language of the dual language book, here would be a nice opportunity to ask them to read/translate a section of the story if they would like. Moreover, if the facilitator has a PENpal Audio Recorder Pen, the children could listen to a reading of the story in English or the other language of the dual language book.

9. Throughout the story, explicitly draw children's attention to the illustrations to promote comprehension of the text.

10. During reading, encourage children to make connections (orally, using mime, in writing). Connections may be *text-to-self* (what does the child notice from the book in relation to his/her own lived experiences), *text-to-text* (what does the child notice from one book/story to another book/story), or *text-to-wider-world* (what does the child notice from the book in relation to real world historical or current contexts).

Discussion to Encourage Reflection and Response:

11. Facilitate discussion with the group of children using literal, inferential, and evaluative questions. The facilitator may wish to select questions from the following list:

Literal Questions:

(Readers use information directly from the text to answer this type of question.)

    i.   *What smell filled the room when the tree was brought inside?*
    ii. *What day can Polish children open their Christmas presents?*
    iii. *Who brought carp to the family?*
    iv. *How many dishes are on the table?*
    v. *When could the family start their supper?*
    vi. *What Christmas carol did Alice play on the recorder?*

Inferential Questions:

(Reader must use the information in the text to deduce the answer.)

    i.   *Why does Marek have a coat in his hand?*
    ii. *Why does dziadek ask for help to bring the tree inside?*
    iii. *Why did the family set an extra space for Christmas Eve supper at the table?*

Evaluative Questions:

(Reader uses his/her own knowledge to explore answers to this type of question.)

    i.   *Which customs/traditions of Polish Christmas do you like best? Why?*
    ii. *Do you think everyone was enjoying themselves when they sang Christmas carols? Why/Why not?*
    iii. *Do you think Alice heard Borys talk?*

Word Identification/Fluency Development:

12. ***Revisit the story and identify key vocabulary words:*** Display key vocabulary words from the story. Reread a section from the story and ask the children to raise their hands when they hear or see one of the key vocabulary words.

13. ***Retell the story (in pairs or small groups):*** Present key words from the story listed in order as they appear in the story. Using the words, children retell the story in small groups or pairs. The facilitator may ask the children to retell the story orally or in writing. The facilitator may present sentences with key words for this activity to provide

the children with additional support. The children could also retell the story using illustrations, mime or still images.

Independent Work/Group Work Activity:

14. ***Listen to Cicha Noc (Silent Night in Polish):*** Before playing *Cicha Noc* to the children, inform the group that you will play a piece of music to them and that you would like them to listen carefully. Tell the children that you would like them to try to identify the instruments they hear playing. Ask the children if they have heard this Christmas carol before. What is similar or different to the version that they heard? Ask the children to identify the language that they think the Christmas carol *Cicha Noc* is being sung in.

15. ***Facilitator in Role & Hot Seating Drama Activity:***
    - A piece of clothing (e.g., hat or scarf) will be needed for this activity in order to signify that the facilitator will assume the role of Marek or Alice from the story.
    - ***Preparation for Facilitator in Role:*** Ask the children to consider what they would ask Marek or Alice about the Christmas traditions celebrated in Poland if they could meet the characters from the story. A "Think/Pair/Share" activity may be useful to help the children formulate questions to ask the characters.
    - ***Facilitator in Role:*** After the children have shared their questions with the whole group, inform the children that when the facilitator is wearing the piece of clothing (i.e., hat or scarf), he/she will assume the role of Marek or Alice.
    - ***Character Hot Seating:*** Wearing the piece of clothing, thank the children for coming to visit their family in Poland. Next, invite the children to ask questions about the Christmas traditions celebrated by Marek and Alice and their family.
    - At the end of this activity, the facilitator will remove the piece of clothing used to signify that he/she has returned from the role of Marek or Alice.

Conclusion:

Facilitate a discussion with the group. Ask the children to explain what they learned about Christmas traditions in Poland. At this point, the facilitator may want to revisit essential questions to determine whether the children have understood the main ideas of the lesson:

- *How is Christmas celebrated in Poland?*
- *What Christmas customs followed by Marek and Alice are similar/different to customs celebrated in your home?*
- *For those children who do not celebrate Christmas, how are some traditions of Polish Christmas similar/different to holidays they celebrate in the winter? What traditions do they have around meal times, gift giving, and singing?*

As a concluding activity, invite the children to discuss these questions with the whole group, in smaller groups, in pairs, or as a written reflection. An activity such as "Two Stars and a Wish" may be a nice conclusion to the lesson. In this activity, children identify two things they have learned and one thing they would like to learn about Christmas in Poland.

Assessment:

Facilitator Observation: Children's engagement and interaction with the lesson, engagement in discussions, and engagement with facilitator designed tasks.

Facilitator Questioning: Higher and lower order questioning (i.e., literal, inferential, and evaluative questions).

Facilitator Designed Tasks: Making predictions, vocabulary games, reading fluency activities, listening and responding to music, drama activity (character hot-seating).

Self-Assessment: "Two Stars and a Wish"

Accommodations/Differentiation:

Differential modes of Representation:

Photos, pictures, flashcards, physical materials (e.g., suitcase), *Cicha Noc* (Silent Night in Polish).

Differential Questioning:

Use of higher and lower order questioning (i.e., literal, inferential, and evaluative questions).

Differential Product/Response:

Written responses, oral responses, music responses to *Cicha Noc* (Silent Night in Polish), drama responses.

In a classroom setting, it may be helpful for the English language learners (ELLs) to take the dual language book home either before or after the lesson. The ELL student may read the book at home in the language spoken by his/her family. This will increase the child's confidence when talking about the book in school. If possible, ask the child's parent/ guardian to read and record the book in the language that he/she speaks at home. The recording could then be played in the classroom, enabling children to hear other languages spoken by their peers at home.

Extension Activities:

Travel Journal Entry (English - Independent Writing Exercise):

The facilitator may wish to extend children's engagement with *Marek and Alice's Christmas* through descriptive writing exercises. If the children "traveled to Poland," encourage them to record the Christmas traditions that they "saw" on their visit. The facilitator may wish to encourage the children to write about similarities and/or differences to the holidays celebrated by their families. Alternatively, children could write Marek or Alice's diary entry. They may focus on a key moment from the story such as Christmas Eve dinner or singing Christmas Carols.

Character Sketch (English – Writing):

Through questioning and discussion, elicit from the children what they know about Marek and Alice, the main characters in the story (e.g., appearance, role in the story, dealing with other characters). Inform the children that they will create a character profile of either Marek or Alice. To assist children to generate ideas for this activity, the facilitator may ask the children to close their eyes and visualize either Marek or Alice. Next, ask each child to draw a sketch of his/her chosen character. Finally, encourage the children to write adjectives or vocabulary words to describe their character.

Drawing 'Photographs' Taken on Journey to Poland (Visual Arts):

Engage in a discussion with the children, asking them to describe what they saw on their "visit" to Poland. Elicit the Christmas traditions the children observed Marek and Alice's family celebrating (e.g., decorating the Christmas tree, looking for the Star of Bethlehem, eating Christmas Eve dinner, singing Christmas carols). Inform the children that they will each create a photograph to illustrate a key moment they observed from their "visit." Ask the children to engage in a Think/Pair/Share activity to discuss possible ideas to draw in their photographs. Moreover, children who do not celebrate Christmas may draw a "photograph" to illustrate customs and traditions associated with a holiday that they celebrate.

Provide the children with coloring materials to carry out the activity. The facilitator may wish to provide children with a simple template (e.g., a rectangular outline bordering a page to indicate that the child's drawing is a photograph). While the children draw the photographs, the facilitator may circulate around the room, offering assistance, providing descriptive feedback, and making suggestions to the children. When the children have finished creating their photographs, ask them to present their completed artworks to the group. Encourage each child to explain which Christmas tradition he/she chose to draw and why he/she drew that particular custom or tradition.

Project Work on Poland (Geography):

Develop the children's map reading skills by locating Poland on a map. Using a large poster/chart, a digital map, or an atlas, ask the children questions to encourage them to examine the physical features of the country. For example, what continent is Poland in? What countries border Poland? Is Poland a landlocked country? What sea borders Poland? Ask the children to name and locate main cities, rivers and mountains in Poland.

Additionally, children could conduct independent research on Poland. Areas of focus for this project work may include:

- **General Information:** Population, capital city, government, language(s), predominant religion, currency, national symbol.
- **Map of Poland:** Indicate physical features such as capital city, bordering seas, islands, mountain ranges, rivers, and lakes. Note interesting facts about the country's geography (e.g., longest river, highest mountain, largest island).
- **Flag of Poland:** Picture/sketch of the flag and information about the flag.
- **Language & Culture:** Identify the language(s) spoken in the country with examples of every day phrases. Identify some of the country's art and culture, customs and traditions, traditional dances and sports.
- **Traditional Food:** Identify examples of traditional dishes, briefly explaining the ingredients.
- **Attractions:** Identify interesting places to visit, tourist attractions, briefly describe the places.
- **Interesting Facts:** Create a "Did you know?" page with some interesting facts learned about the country (e.g., identify a famous person who was born in Poland).
- **Craft:** Make a craft/item to represent something from the country's culture. For example, make a traditional dish or construct a famous landmark.
- **Similarities and Differences:** Children identify similarities and differences between Poland and where they live or their countries of birth.

Vocabulary Flashcards for *Marek and Alice's Christmas*:

pine tree	carp	Star of Bethlehem
Blessed bread	recorder	Silent Night
St. Nicolas' Day	Midnight Mass	offer wishes
greeted	fast	doorbell
hay	Jesus	stable
quad bike	carols	wrapping presents
unpack	welcome	Christmas tree
Christmas decorations	prayer	present
star	sing	supper
chips	extra plate	

DIVERSITY ACTIVITIES TO PROMOTE MULTICULTURALISM

"It is not our differences that divide us. It is our inability to recognize, accept, and celebrate those differences."
- Audre Lorde

This section provides educators with numerous ideas to support multiculturalism. The activities and games in this section can teach all children about diverse cultures and languages while also helping immigrant children feel pride in their heritage.

Here you can find the following:

- Simple ways to use bilingual books to promote literacy and language awareness
- 10 games from around the world
- 10 language learning games to play with bilingual books
- Multicultural craft ideas and foods from around the world
- Language profiles to introduce language diversity
- Unique Holidays to Promote Multiculturalism and Literacy

Teachers can pick and choose from the activities presented here to promote diversity and build community in the classroom. The games can also be incorporated cross-curricularly throughout the year. For example, the crafts from around the world could be made in an art unit, the more active games from different countries could be played in physical education classes, and students can enjoy the literacy games in Language Arts classes. Celebrating special events (e.g., Celebrating the Bilingual Child Month) with foods from around the world is another way to build community.

10 Simple Ways to Use Bilingual Books to Promote Literacy and Language Awareness

Research on child development consistently shows that ongoing support of a child's home language is essential in supporting his/her academic progress. Parents who interact with their children in their native tongue through conversation, day-to-day activities, and reading to them out loud help their children academically, even if the language spoken at school is different from the native language spoken at home.

For dual-language families, bilingual books can be very helpful in providing a bridge between the two languages. They offer educators a chance to teach children in the language spoken at school, while fostering an appreciation for the language spoken at home. Bilingual books encourage parents to continue using their home language, knowing that it will benefit, not detract from, their children's school language learning.

Here are 10 tips to help parents and teachers use bilingual books at home and in the classroom to advance language skills as well as to encourage cultural appreciation:

1. **Teachers read the bilingual book out loud in the school language while parents read the same book out loud at home in the home language.** Parents who read to their children in a home language actually strengthen their children's academic skills. This is in addition to many other benefits, such as enhancing the parent-child bond through shared language and culture.

2. **Teachers read bilingual books in the school language and show the words written in the other language.** Teachers can use bilingual books to introduce students to languages that use the Roman alphabet as well as to languages such as Arabic and Chinese that use different symbols and characters. Seeing that languages can be written using a variety of letters and scripts helps children understand that sounds and words can be represented in diverse ways. As the teacher reads the bilingual book aloud, she can point out the different words or symbols in the second language.

3. **Read bilingual books that highlight different cultures.** When teachers select bilingual books that focus on different cultures, traditions, and customs, they are helping children feel comfortable with cultural diversity. It is a gentle way for teachers to cultivate multicultural awareness and appreciation in their students.

4. **While reading the story in the school language, pick out a few key words in the other language.** The idea here is to stimulate curiosity and interest in language, not to confuse the students, so it should be kept to a minimum. By periodically using words from other languages, the teacher shows the dual-language students in the classroom that an effort is being made to understand their languages. It indicates that the students' languages are of value and worth learning.

5. **Parents or volunteers read bilingual books to the class in their languages.** Ask parents of the students to volunteer to read a bilingual book in their language(s) out loud to the class. Afterward, the teacher can read the same book out loud in the school language. This strengthens an appreciation of family and community in the classroom, and provides parents the opportunity to offer something in which they are experts: their language(s). If parents are unwilling or cannot volunteer, reach out to other teachers who know the language and can read the book out loud.

6. **Encourage students to write their own bilingual books.** After reading a number of bilingual books out loud, work with dual-language students to help them create their own bilingual books. They will feel empowered by the fact that they can speak more than one language. Even if they can't read or write yet, teachers and parents can work together with the student to write down the words in each language while the child provides the pictures for each page.

7. **Allow children to pick out bilingual books from the school or public library.** Having the option to select books is very empowering. Teachers and parents should contact their school and local libraries to find out if they have bilingual books available to borrow. Teachers can also develop classroom "lending libraries" with bilingual books. The benefit of having children pick out bilingual books is that both family members and teachers can engage with children using the same books.

8. **Ask questions and encourage discussion in both languages.** Bilingual books provide the opportunity for discussion on the same topic in more than one language. Teachers can promote discussion in the school language while parents can encourage it in their home language. Teachers can send home a list of discussion topics for parents to utilize at home if they wish. Meanwhile, parents should feel encouraged to share conversations from home about the target bilingual books with their child's teacher.

9. **Encourage children to read bilingual books in both languages.** If children can read in both languages, they should be encouraged to do so, even if one language is stronger than the other. In fact, understanding the story in the stronger language can promote comprehension in the weaker language. Teachers and parents can help this language transfer by encouraging students to read the stories as much as possible in each language.

10. **Bilingual books provide an opportunity to have fun with language.** Having fun with languages is an important part of language learning and utilization. Bilingual books provide a springboard for this on many different levels. Discussing the various topics, the words, the different written scripts, and the "unusual" letters in a language's alphabet are just a few ways teachers can make languages fun and exciting for their students. Parents can help their children learn about the school language by asking questions about words, pronunciation, and more in the bilingual books that their children bring home. In an effort to reach language mastery, enjoyment is an important ingredient for language success.

These are just a few ideas on how to use bilingual books with children in the classroom and at home. The goal is to help children embrace all of their languages so that as they grow they will be able to use these languages with confidence in the many multilingual and multicultural situations in which they may find themselves. Reading and enjoying bilingual books is one great way to help children achieve this goal.

10 Games from Around the World

Multicultural games are a great way to teach children about other countries and cultures while still having fun. Some of these games just need a few people, while others can be played with large groups. They are simple to learn and do not require a lot of equipment. Children of all ages can join in and stay active while simultaneously learning something new.

Hunters and Rabbits (Belgium)

Play this game with any number of people in a wide, open place.

- One player starts with the ball – he/she is the hunter. This player then has to dribble the ball to get closer to the "rabbits," which is everyone else in the game.
- The rabbits are only allowed to hop, they cannot run.
- Once the hunter gets close enough to a rabbit, he/she must stop and roll the ball towards a rabbit's feet. If the ball touches the rabbit, then that rabbit becomes a hunter too. If the ball lands anywhere else, then the rabbit stays a rabbit.
- The last rabbit standing is the winner of the game. The tricky part is that no matter how many hunters there are, there can only be one ball to catch the rabbits with.

Hoops (Greece)

This game requires at least 5 people on each team, 2 hula hoops, and small balls (or bean bags).

- There are two teams, and each team selects one person to be the Roller. The Roller will stand at the starting line with a hula hoop.
- The rest of the players will be on the side with small balls or bean bags.
- The Roller rolls the hula hoop past the people on their team, and they try to get as many balls through the hoop as possible without the balls touching the hoop.
- The team that is able to get the most balls through the hoop is the winner.

Goellki (Russia)

This simple game requires no props and can be played anywhere there is some room to run.

- Players stand in pairs, with one pair behind the other.
- One player stands behind the row of pairs and that person is "it."
- The person designated as "it" then yells "Go!" and the last pair in line must run to the front of the line. One player runs on the left side of the line the other on the right, and they need to reach the front without being tagged by "it."
- If "it" is unable to tag anyone then he or she must be "it" again for the next round and the runners wait at the front of the line. However, if "it" does tag somebody then the person tagged is the new "it" and the previous "it" goes to the front of the line.
- The game continues with the new pair at the back becoming the runners.

Reloj (Peru)

Play the "Clock" game with up to 14 players with a long jump rope. Two of the 14 players will be spinning the jump rope while the other players line up.

- The first player in line jumps into the rope, jumps once, and comes out without being hit by the rope.
- Then the next player runs in and jumps twice and comes out.
- This pattern continues up until 12 jumps in a row.
- Once the players reach 12 jumps, the pattern will start with 1 again.
- Note: There must be no hesitation to run and jump into the rope; if there is, then that player is out. Also if a player hits the rope at any time with any part of his or her body, the player will also be out.
- The last jumper standing is the winner.

El Gato y El Raton (Puerto Rico)

"The Cat and the Mouse" game is played with a group of people who choose a leader. (Typically the leader is an adult.)

- The leader will select one person to be the cat and one person to be the mouse. The rest of the people will form a circle holding hands.
- The mouse will start on the inside of the circle and the cat will start on the outside. The objective is for the cat to catch the mouse with the people in the circle trying to help the mouse escape and keep the cat out without ever unlocking arms.
- If the cat gets into the circle, the mouse must escape it.

- When the mouse is caught, the leader chooses two new people to be cat and mouse, and the game starts all over again.

Stalker (Botswana)

One of the characters in this enjoyable group game is an animal native to southern and southwestern Africa. The springbok is a graceful, medium-sized antelope that sprints quickly through arid plains.

- Two players are chosen to be the Hunter and the Springbok. These two players are blind-folded and the rest of the players form a circle around them.
- The Hunter must try to catch the Springbok, and the Springbok tries to stay away from the Hunter. The group is not allowed to touch either player, but they may choose to make different animal noises to distract the Hunter.
- Once the Springbok is caught, the group chooses two new people to be the Hunter and the Springbok.

Catching Stars (Equatorial Guinea, Zaire)

This game is typically played with a large number of players.

- Split the group into one smaller group and one bigger group. The smaller group is made up of Catchers and the bigger group is made up of Stars.
- All the Stars stand in a line on one side of the field, and the Catchers stand spread out in the middle.
- The Catchers say, "star light, star bright, how many stars are out tonight?" The Stars respond, "more than you can catch!" The Stars then try to run as quickly as possible to the other side of the field without being tagged by the Catchers.
- If Stars are tagged by Catchers, they become Catchers too. The game continues until all Stars become Catchers.

1, 2, 3 Dragon! (China)

This is an active group game that is fun for children of all ages.

- Players form a line with each player's hands on the shoulders of the person in front of them. The first person in line is the Head, and the last person in line is the Tail.
- The Tail yells, "1, 2, 3 dragon!" and the Head starts moving to try to catch the Tail. The rest of the players must follow the Head's movements exactly, while staying connected to one another.

- If the line disconnects, then the dragon has died, and the Head must move to the end of the line to become the Tail. If the Head is able to catch the Tail, the dragon survives!
- The Head still moves to the back of the line to become the Tail in order to give the next person in line a chance to be the Head.

Palm Ball (Italy)

Similar to Four Square in the US, this game requires a ball and a piece of chalk.

- Draw a big rectangle on the ground with chalk and draw a line through the center of the rectangle. Each player stands in one side of the box.
- One player starts by serving the ball into the other person's box, and that player must send the ball back by hitting it.
- Players can't hold the ball - they can only hit it back into the other person's box. The ball can only bounce in the box twice before making it to the other side.

Triangle Game (Greece)

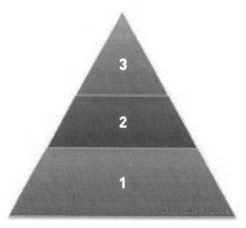

This game is typically played outside with a small group of people.

- Draw a large triangle on the ground with chalk and split it into 3 parts as shown above. The smallest part is labeled with a 3, the middle a 2 and the bottom a 1.
- Players take turns throwing rocks from 15 feet away. As they are throwing, the players add up their scores based on the numbered section that the rock landed in.
- The first person to 50 is the winner.

For more games from around the world, we recommend *Multicultural Games* by Lorraine Barbarash (1997).

10 Language Learning Games to Play with Bilingual Books

Using flash cards and rote learning to teach an additional language is like looking at pictures of a turkey dinner instead of sitting down to eat the wonderful meal. There are so many more interesting ways to experience learning and using a new language, and bilingual books are a great place to start.

Students who are learning English or a foreign language can use the words and pictures in books to play simple games that build language skills while having fun. Such games not only support language retention in an enjoyable way, they can also build community and cooperation among students. The following games vary in terms of necessary levels of proficiency.

Charades

This classic game works really well to help cement children's understanding of the bilingual books they've recently read. Children can choose a favorite character from the story to act out with gestures and no words. However, to really improve their vocabulary, choosing *objects* from the book for their peers to identify in the target language will push them one step further in their language-learning.

You Be the Star

For this activity, children choose a favorite scene from the bilingual book they are reading and act it out for each other. They should use as many words in the new language as they can to get across the main idea, even if they are not using dialogue and narrative lifted straight from the page.

Key Word Shuffle

This game is a real vocabulary-builder. Using index cards or squares of construction paper, list a number of key words in the new language from the selected bilingual books. For example, the story of Cinderella might produce key words like *prince, pumpkin, glass slipper*, and *sweep*. Shuffle the cards and let the children choose them at random and then find the page in the book that contains the word.

Scavenger Hunt

With more time and resources, build on the Key Word Shuffle by allowing young children to search for bilingual treasures. They can use index cards with words in the language they are learning as clues to find objects from a story in the home or classroom. For example, when reading the bilingual version of *Goldilocks and the Three Bears*, children can hunt for chairs, bowls, or even a box of instant porridge!

Memory Game

Children love puzzles at any age, and this quick game will challenge their memories *and* the language they have learned so far. It is simple: copy the pages of a bilingual story, shuffle them, and ask the children to put them back in order without looking at the book. For children who need a little more support, copy only a few of the most important pages from the plot. If the students are a bit more advanced, let them try the whole thing.

Pictionary

It is fun, fast-paced, and focuses children's minds on new-language vocabulary they are learning. Just like in the game show from the 1990s, this version uses key words and phrases from bilingual stories the children are familiar with. The twist is that they *must* guess in the target language. The competitive element will add excitement and keep children involved in their learning long after they have shut their books for the day.

Puppet Show

This puppet show activity combines arts and crafts and bilingual learning. Children can spend time making creative puppets to represent characters from the book they are reading before using them to act out a scene with lines of memorized dialogue in the target language. Encourage students to take home the puppets and share what they have learned.

The Post-it Note Game

Some sticky notes, a pen, and a bilingual children's book are the ingredients for the Post-it Note game. This version requires a little bit more knowledge of the new language but it is great fun once students have advanced to this level. Simply write the names of characters (or objects, to make it even more challenging) from the story onto Post-it Notes. Then stick them to the foreheads of the players so they can only read the Post-it Notes of the people at whom they are looking and not their own. The children then ask yes-or-no questions to try to figure out "who" they are, such as, "Am I a girl or a boy? Do I have dark hair? Do I climb a beanstalk? Am I bigger than everyone else in the story?" The higher their level of proficiency, the better questions they can ask, adding to the fun of the game.

Hot Seating

A complex role-playing game, this will really test young learners' vocabulary. To play, children take turns performing as a character from the bilingual book they have read, while the others ask them questions about how they felt at different points in the story. As in the Post-it Note Game, the better their skills in their new language, the better the questions they can ask, and the deeper they can go exploring the emotions and characters in the text. For instance, if students are reading *Marek and Alice's Christmas*, they can use the additional language to ask questions like "How did you feel about visiting Poland for Christmas? What were you expecting Christmas to be like? Why do you like spending time with your babcia? What was your favorite part of Christmas?" Let children be creative with this activity, but the closer they can stay to the text the more they will be reinforcing what they have already learned. *See the lesson plans in Section 2 for more examples of this activity.*

What Happens Next?

The end of a really good story is always a bit disappointing — the reader wishes the author had carried on. In this game, children can do just that by adding an epilogue or sequel to the bilingual book they have read. Learners will need to be able to use their new language to a high level to get involved in this activity, but even a very simple continuation of the story can be fun, satisfying, and an effortless way to reinforce language skills.

This is just a small selection of the games teachers and parents can use to support bilingualism. Consider adapting other popular games to support language learning.

Creating Multicultural Crafts

Bring cultural diversity and international flavor to the classroom with simple crafts. The crafts below can all be made with readily available materials. Plus, they involve minimal mess and are simple enough for most children to complete on their own.

The first five crafts listed here can be used when exploring harvest festivals around the world. While Thanksgiving is a great time to introduce these crafts to a classroom, keep in mind that harvest festivals are not always in November. Typically they coincide with a country's seasons and the kind of crop they are harvesting.

The next four crafts use music to introduce children to different cultures. As Henry Wadsworth Longfellow said, "Music is the universal language of mankind." It can evoke emotions that are at the heart of the shared human experience. These crafts celebrate diversity and remind us of what we all have in common.

The crafts listed in this section are just starting points. More craft ideas are available online. Images of the crafts listed below can be found at the following links:

https://blog.languagelizard.com/2014/11/19/5-kid-crafts-that-add-multicultural-traditions-to-your-thanksgiving/
https://blog.languagelizard.com/2018/08/20/4-musical-multicultural-kid-crafts/

India: Pongal – Kolam Chalk Drawings

Pongal, the harvest festival of Southern India, is celebrated in January or February. It celebrates the successful harvest of rice, sugarcane, and turmeric. Kolam drawings are traditionally symmetrical and placed in front of doors. These drawings are believed to bring happiness and prosperity. This activity requires only colored chalk and clear weather.

Israel: Sukkot – CD Suncatchers

The festival of *Sukkot*, celebrated in September or October, is a time to remember the culture's agricultural roots. The holiday centers around a special kind of dwelling called a "sukkah," which has a roof of organic material, like palm leaves. The inside of the sukkah is strung with bright, shiny decorations. Make this craft with old, scratched CDs, and anything shiny and colorful.

Vietnam: Mid-Autumn Festival – Lanterns

The *Mid-Autumn Festival* celebrates a successful harvest and also honors children. Children get special lanterns and take part in a parade. Lanterns can be made from paper and tape, and children can organize a parade at home.

Portugal: Madeira Flower Festival – Headbands & Hats

The *Madeira Flower Festival* takes place in the spring, when flowers are in bloom. The festival features a parade with floats and flowers everywhere, especially worn on clothing. Children can make flowers out of any material available: gift wrap, tissue paper, colored paper, paper towels, or scraps of fabric. The flowers can be secured with pipe cleaner, tape, yarn, or rubber bands onto headbands, hats, belts, or any article of clothing. If the weather is nice, the children can have a parade, in true Flower Festival spirit.

United Kingdom: Harvest Festival – Corn Husk Dolls

The *UK's Harvest Festival* happens in September or October, and includes singing and decorating churches with baskets of food. One traditional harvest time craft is making corn husk dolls. If corn husks are not available, scraps of fabric are an easy substitute. Once completed, children can make hair from yarn and clothes from felt.

Peru: Panpipes (*Zampoña*)

Panpipes (also known as panflutes) are one of the earliest known musical instruments in the Americas. The oldest was discovered in Peru, and dates back to 4200 BC. Make a child-friendly version of this woodwind instrument by cutting straws to different lengths and taping them to pieces of cardboard. Gently blow across the tops, and enjoy the soft, echoing sounds.

China: Pellet Drums (*Bo Lang Gu*)

Pellet drums (also known as rattle drums) originated in China around 300 B.C. as an instrument used during banquets and religious celebrations. It is now generally known for its use by street vendors and as a children's toy. Children can make their own pellet drums with two paper plates, yarn, beads, and a craft stick. Just twist the rod back and forth so the pellets strike each side of the drum.

South America / Africa / China: Rain Sticks

A number of ancient civilizations used ceremonial rain sticks to call for rain. The origin of the first rain stick is unknown. (Some say it originated in South America, others say Africa or China.) They can be made from a paper towel roll pierced with a few toothpicks. Fill it with beads or dry beans, close off the ends, and enjoy the peaceful tap-tapping sound of rain.

Australia: Clapsticks (*Bilma*)

Clapsticks, or *bilma*, are an instrument used in Aboriginal ceremonies in Australia. Traditionally made of hard eucalyptus wood, they make a hard, rapping sound when struck together. Children can make clapsticks from short sections of PVC pipe and then dance to their wonderful rhythm.

Celebrating with Foods from Around the World

Think of any holiday celebrated in any part of the world, and there is sure to be at least one traditional dish associated with it. Thanksgiving turkey, corned beef on St. Patrick's Day, or rice cakes for Chinese New Year... food is the cornerstone of any celebration.

Food also offers a great way to learn about a culture's identity, stories, and history. For example, sweets are eaten during Diwali to symbolize the defeat of evil and the triumph of goodness and light. Introducing foods from around the world provides an opportunity to both celebrate together and teach about other cultures. It also helps children open up and talk about their own family's culinary traditions.

Below are several delicious winter holiday dishes from around the world. Let this help start your culinary journey, but don't end here. Consider hosting a classroom potluck lunch where everyone can join in and introduce the foods from their heritage. Or, if individual foods are introduced, follow up the meal with a storybook from the same part of the world. Children will have an experience that nourishes the body and the mind.

Images and links to the recipes for the foods below are available at this link: https://blog.languagelizard.com/2014/12/16/celebrate-holiday-diversity-foods-around-world-international/

India – Gulab Jamun

In India, Diwali is the winter holiday known as the Festival of Lights. One tradition is to give sweets to friends and neighbors. Gulab Jamun, which translates to "rose berries," are deep fried dough balls covered in rose water-scented syrup.

Japan – Udon Noodle Soup

It is believed that udon noodles were first brought to Japan from China in the 9th century by Buddhist monks. Udon noodles, made from wheat flour, are thick and chewy. They can be served in a variety of ways: cold or hot, with sauce, or stir-fried. Its neutral flavor matches well with a variety of ingredients. In Japan's cold winter months, hot udon noodle soup is a popular comfort food. To eat udon the traditional way, use chopsticks and show appreciation with an enthusiastic slurping sound.

Mexico – Tamales

Tamales have been eaten in what is now known as Central America since before 5,000 B.C. They quickly grew in popularity due to their portability and the way they can fill the belly. Made from masa dough that is filled with meats, cheese, or vegetables, tamales are wrapped in a corn husk, then steamed or boiled. They are traditionally made during the holidays, because tamales take many hands to assemble, and are cooked in huge batches.

Germany – Speckknoedel (or Speckknödel)

Speckknoedel are the dumplings of Europe's mountainous Alpine region. They were probably invented and then gained popularity as a winter food because they enabled people to stretch ever-dwindling meat and bread supplies in the cold months.

Mongolia – Buuz

Mongolian Lunar New Year, known as Tsagaan Sar, is considered one of the culture's most important holidays. It is a time of year dedicated to family and feasts. Warm meat- and vegetable-filled dumplings called Buuz are a popular and delicious holiday treat.

Introducing Diverse Languages

In this section, we provide a brief overview and some interesting facts about 11 different languages around the world: Arabic, Chinese, Farsi, French, German, Hindi, Japanese, Nepali, Russian, Somali, and Spanish. We also include the image of a page from a bilingual book for each language to show different language scripts.

Share this information to help students appreciate linguistic differences. These overviews can be used as a springboard to encourage students to learn about other languages or to delve more deeply into the languages represented in their classroom.

Note: Except where otherwise noted, the U.S. language speaker data in this section is taken from 2016 estimates of the U.S. Census Bureau's American Community Survey (ASC).

Arabic

أراد ألفي أن يكون ملاكاً.
كان قد رآهم في كتبه.

Alfie wanted to be an angel.
He'd seen them in his books.

كان قد رآهم في أحلامه.

He'd seen them in his dreams.

Where is Arabic Spoken?

Arabic is spoken in a very large area that includes North Africa, the Arabian Peninsula, and parts of the Middle East. About 185 million people speak it around the world. Arabic has many features in common with the Hebrew and Amharic languages. Muslims consider Arabic to be the divine language of Allah.

There are about one million Arabic speakers in the U.S. There are large Arabic speaking populations in New York, California, New Jersey, and Washington, D.C.

Interesting Facts About Arabic

- Arabic is written and read from right to left, and each symbol represents a letter.
- Formal Classical Arabic, also called Literary Arabic or Fusha, is learned by every Arabic speaker. There are numerous local vernacular forms of Arabic. Dialects can differ greatly from each other in both vocabulary and sounds used.
- The Arabic version of *Sesame Street* uses Fusha.

Chinese

一条有红色鳍金色眼的小鱼儿，伊善最初认识他时，他的确是很细小的。
但她用食物和爱心喂养小鱼，他很快便逐渐长成一条巨大的鱼。
每当伊善来到池塘时，鱼儿总是把他的头伸起来枕在她旁边的池畔。
没有人知道伊善的秘密，直至有一天她的继母问自己的女儿。
「究竟伊善拿着她的米饭跑到那里去呢？」
她的女儿谦说说：「你为什么不跟踪她看看？」

于是，雅每躲在一丛芦苇后面，等候着，观察着，当她看到伊善离去时，
她把手伸进水池来回搅动，「鱼啊！鱼啊！」她低声吟哦，但是鱼儿
安然留在水底，「可恶的家伙，」继母咒骂着说，「我会将你…」

...a tiny fish with red fins and golden eyes. At least, he was tiny when Yeh-hsien first found him. But she nourished her fish with food and with love, and soon he grew to an enormous size. Whenever she visited her pond the fish always raised his head out of the water and rested it on the bank beside her. No one knew her secret. Until, one day, the stepmother asked her daughter. "Where does Yeh-hsien go with her grains of rice?" "Why don't you follow her?" suggested the daughter, "and find out."

So, behind a clump of reeds, the stepmother waited and watched. When she saw Yeh-hsien leave, she thrust her hand into the pool and thrashed it about. "Fish! Oh fish!" she crooned. But the fish stayed safely underwater. "Wretched creature," the stepmother cursed. "I'll get you..."

Where is Chinese spoken?

Mandarin and Cantonese are the largest Chinese dialects. Mandarin (sometimes referred to as Standard Chinese) is the official language of China, Taiwan, and Singapore. Nearly one billion people around the world speak Mandarin, more than any other language.

Cantonese (sometimes referred to as Traditional Chinese) is spoken in Hong Kong, Macau, Guangzhou, and around the area of Canton, in southern China. There about 80 million Cantonese speakers in the world. Chinese people living overseas more frequently speak Cantonese than Mandarin.

There are over three million Chinese language speakers (of all varieties and dialects) in the U.S. That is close to a 300 percent increase since the 1980 Census. There are large Chinese language speaking populations in New York, California, Texas, and New Jersey. There are about as many Mandarin speakers as Cantonese speakers in the U.S., and also many residents who speak other dialects.

Interesting Facts About Chinese Languages

- Mandarin and Cantonese are both tonal languages, meaning intonation and pitch affect the meaning of words.
- Chinese languages have no verb conjugation, gender-specific nouns, or tenses (past, present, future).
- "Pinyin" is a method of writing Mandarin words using the Roman alphabet.

Farsi

Where is Farsi spoken?

Farsi, also known as Persian, Dari, or Tajiki, is the national language of Iran, Afghanistan, and Tajikistan. It is also spoken in other parts of the Middle East and India. There are around 60 to 80 million native speakers around the world.

There are about 400,000 people who speak Farsi in the U.S. There are large Farsi speaking populations in California, New York, and Washington, D.C.

Interesting Facts About Farsi

- Farsi has twenty-three consonants and six vowel sounds. It is written from right to left. (Numerals are written from left to right.)
- In Farsi, nouns have no gender, and there are no articles. Farsi is considered to have a relatively simple grammatical structure.
- The first handwritten book in Farsi was a medical book written in 1055.

French

"Viens Mère, j'ai un plan," a répondu sa fille, et elle partit dans le jardin. Là, elle cueillit la plus grosse courge qu'elle trouva, coupa le haut et la creusa.

"Come Mother, I have a plan," answered the daughter, and went into the garden. There, she picked the largest marrow she could find, cut off the top and hollowed it out.

"Monte dedans. Puis, je pousserai la courge et elle te roulera jusqu'à la maison. Au revoir Mère."
"Au revoir ma fille," a répondu la vieille femme tout en l'étreignant.

"Climb in. Then, I'll push the marrow, and it will roll you home. Goodbye Mother."
"Goodbye Daughter," answered the old woman, as they hugged each other.

Where is French spoken?

French is the official language of France, and it is one of the most widely spoken languages in the world. There are about 300 million French speakers worldwide, including many in Canada and several African countries. It has official status in 32 countries, second only to English.

There are over 1.2 million French speakers in the U.S. (including Cajun). There are large French speaking populations in New York, Louisiana, Washington D.C., Massachusetts, Texas, and California.

Interesting Facts About French

- There are many food-related idioms in French. One example is "En faire tout un fromage," which translates to "make a whole cheese of it." This saying is used when a person is making a bigger deal of something than it deserves. In English, its equivalent is "making a mountain out of a molehill."
- While the language was used by the aristocracy before the French Revolution, French as we know it only become widely used in France after the late 1700s.
- "Salut" can be used as both a casual hello or good-bye.

179

German

Kaum hatte sich Little Red vom Schrecken erholt, fiel ihr der arme Sly ein, auf den ein Haufen Ärger wartete. Wie könnte sie ihm nur helfen?

When Little Red had recovered she thought about poor Sly and all the trouble he would be in. What could she do to help?

Where is German spoken?

German is the official language of Germany, Austria, and Liechtenstein, as well as being one of the official languages of Luxembourg and Switzerland. There are around 90 million German speakers around the world, making it the 11th most-spoken language globally.

There are close to one million German speakers in the U.S., with large German speaking populations along the East Coast, as well as in California and Illinois.

Interesting Facts About German

- There are 30 letters in the German alphabet. The umlaut (the dots over the letters ä, ö, ü) changes a word's pronunciation.
- German nouns have three genders: masculine, feminine, and gender-neutral.
- When meeting someone new, you should use "sie" (the formal "you") until invited to use the informal "du."

Hindi

उस रात जब सभी सो रहे थे चोर चुपके से गाँव में घुस गया।
"यहीं वह घर है," एक फुसफुसाया।
"नहीं, वह यहाँ है," दूसरे ने कहा।
"तुम क्या कह रहे हो? वह यहाँ है," एक तीसरा चोर चिल्लाया।
कईद चकरा गया। कुछ बहुत बड़ी गड़बड़ हो गयी है, और उसने चोरों को वापस चलने को कहा।

That night the thieves silently entered the village when everyone was fast asleep.
"Here is the house," whispered one.
"No, here it is," said another.
"What are you saying? It is here," cried a third thief.
Ka-eed was confused. Something had gone terribly wrong, and he ordered his thieves to retreat.

Where is Hindi spoken?

Hindi is the official language of India (along with English). Hindi is one of the most widely spoken languages in the world. There are approximately 425 million speakers worldwide.

There are over 700,000 Hindi speakers in the U.S. There are large Hindi speaking populations in New York, New Jersey, Chicago, Washington D.C., and California.

Interesting Facts About Hindi

- Hindi is a relatively easy language to read. It is written left to right, is phonetic, and doesn't include articles like "a" or "the."
- It is important to use the correct formal or informal style of speech in context, depending on whom you are addressing.
- Nouns are either masculine or feminine, and affect adjective and verb use.
- The most common greeting in Hindi is "namaste," and handshakes are only used in certain situations, not in everyday life.

181

Japanese

Where is Japanese spoken?

Japanese is the national language of Japan, and there are approximately 125 million speakers worldwide. Its origins are unknown, and it has no known linguistic relatives. There are dozens of dialects spoken in Japan, but the main distinctions are between Tokyo-type and Kyoto-Osaka-type.

There are approximately 450,000 Japanese speakers in the U.S. There are large Japanese-speaking populations in California, Washington, New York, and Washington D.C.

Interesting Facts About Japanese

- Modern Japanese began around 1600. It has a large number of "borrowed words" from the Chinese language (words of Chinese origin). In the last 50 years, the number of borrowed words from the English language has grown considerably, especially words that are technology related. For example, *intānetto* for "internet." Borrowed words can also be shortened, like *wāpuro* for "word processor."
- The writing system consists primarily of three scripts: kanji, hiragana, and katakana.
- Japanese writings can be in "western style," which is in horizontal rows starting from the top, or "Japanese style," vertical columns starting from the right.

Nepali

तेसपछि पानिघोडाले पनि उनिहर जस्तै गरि कुदने कोशिश गर्यो । तर त्यो सजिलो थिएन ।

Then Hippopotamus tried to do the same.
It wasn't easy.

पानिघोडा "धड्च्याङ" गरि पछारियो चितुवा सरह भई कुदन उसलाई धेरै लामो समय लाग्ने रहेछ ।

Hippopotamus fell down with a CRASH!
It would be a long time before he could
keep up with Cheetah.

Where is Nepali spoken?

Nepali is the official language of Nepal, a country in South Asia. It is also spoken in Bhutan, Burma (Republic of the Union of Myanmar), and India. There are about 17 million Nepali speakers around the world.

There are relatively large Nepalese communities in New York, California, Texas, and Washington D.C. According to the U.S. Census Bureau's 2015 estimate, about 140,000 people in the U.S. identify as Nepalese.

Interesting Facts About Nepali

- In the past, Nepali was called the Khas language and Gorkhali.
- One of the most well-known words in Nepali is "namaste," which means hello. It is usually spoken with a slight bow and palms pressed together. It can be used as a greeting or a goodbye. It is interesting to note that "namaste" is a common greeting in several languages

Russian

Проводил отбор Шакал, каждый участник показывал, на что он способен.
Первой Шакал отобрал Обезьянку, потому что она *всегда* во всем была первой.

Jackal looked on as every creature tried their best.
She chose Monkey first as Monkey *always* won.

Никто не взял в свою команду Ленивца. Это же были спортивные соревнования, а не соревнования по лени.

Nobody chose Sloth.
There was no race for hanging about.

Where is Russian spoken?

Russian is the national language of Russia, as well as Belarus, Kazakhstan, and Kyrgyz-stan. It is also widely used in other European countries like Ukraine, Latvia, and Estonia. Russian is one of the most widely spoken languages in the world. There are approximately 260 million speakers worldwide. It is one of six official languages of the United Nations.

There are just over 900,000 Russian speakers in the U.S., with large Russian speaking populations in New York, New Jersey, California, Washington, and Oregon.

Interesting Facts About Russian

- In the mid-1700s, there were three recognized styles of written Russian: low, middle, and high. Low style was used in everyday correspondence, middle style for prose and poetry, and high style for poetry and religion. Ultimately, middle style became the standard Russian of today.
- The Russian language also makes use of patronyms, which convey lineage by using the names of male ancestors. A person's first name is combined with a form of his/her father's name and -ovich (son of) or -ovna (daughter of) is added onto the end. For example, if Natasha's father's name is Ivan, you would address her as Natasha Ivanovna.

Somali

Where is Somali spoken?

Somali is a part of the Afro-Asiatic language family. Somali is spoken by an estimated 16 million people around the world. It is the official language of Somalia, with several regional dialects, and is also spoken in nearby countries, like Kenya and Ethiopia.

According to 2015 UN estimates, there are about 150,000 Somalis (refugees and non-refugees) living in the U.S. More Somalis live in Minnesota than any other state. There are also large Somali speaking populations in Ohio, Washington, California, and Washington, D.C.

Interesting Facts About Somali

- There are multiple writing systems used to express the Somali language, including an Arabic script (referred to as Wadaad's writing), the Osmanya alphabet, and a Latin script.
- The Latin alphabet is the most commonly used and was formally adopted as the official writing script in Somalia in 1972.
- The Somali language has 20 distinct vowel sounds. It is spoken with three different tones (high, low, and falling) that indicate things like gender and number.

Spanish

Pero la curiosidad es arma de doble filo y a pesar de todo el bien que hacía, Pandora no conseguía sacarse de la cabeza la existencia de la caja. Cada día se iba a verla y recordaba las palabras de Zeus: "¡Esta caja nunca debe ser abierta!"

Después de algunos meses Pandora se encontró sentada frente a la caja una vez más. "¿Qué mal puedo hacer si la abro un poco y veo lo que hay adentro?" se preguntó Pandora. "¿Qué puede haber en la caja que sea tan terrible?" Entonces se cercioró de que no la miraba nadie y con una horquilla de pelo abrió cuidadosamente la cerradura.

But curiosity is a double-edged sword and for all the good that Pandora had done she could not put the locked box out of her mind. Every day she would just go and have a look at it. And every day she remembered Zeus' words: "This box must never be opened!"

After some months had passed Pandora found herself sitting in front of the box again. "What harm would it do if I just sneaked a look inside?" she asked herself. "After all what could possibly be in there that is so terrible?" She looked around to make sure that she was alone and then she took a pin from her hair and carefully picked the lock.

Where is Spanish spoken?

Spanish is spoken by an estimated 560 million people around the world. It is the official language of Spain and Mexico, as well as 20 other countries. It is the second most commonly used language in the world.

According to Instituto Cervantes data, there are about 41 million native Spanish speakers in the U.S., and another 11 million who are bilingual. There are large Spanish speaking populations in New Mexico, California, Texas, and Arizona. There are currently more Spanish speakers in the U.S. than in Spain. In fact, only Mexico surpasses the U.S. in terms of the number of Spanish speakers.

Interesting Facts About Spanish

- In some parts of the world, Spanish is referred to as "español" or "castellano."
- The rolled "r" sound is one of the most challenging aspects of learning to speak Spanish.
- In many Spanish-speaking countries, when greeting informally, it is common to kiss on each cheek.

Unique Holidays to Promote Multiculturalism and Literacy

There are many interesting holidays and festivals that teachers can explore with students to teach them about diverse cultures. It is particularly rewarding when children participate in lessons about the holidays that they celebrate in their homes, or when a parent is willing to teach the class about a holiday from his or her culture.

In addition to teaching about multicultural celebrations such as Chinese New Year, Diwali, Holi, Ramadan, and Cinco de Mayo, educators can use one known holiday to introduce how different cultures celebrate a similar event. For example, in the winter students can learn about New Year celebrations around the world, gaining an understanding that not every culture celebrates the new year at the same time or in the same way. Similarly, in autumn, when chiildren are thinking about Halloween and Thanksgiving, they can learn about related festivals centered on the dead (e.g., Day of the Dead) or celebrating the harvest (e.g., Sukkot). They can also explore the history of those holidays around the world.

In this section we explore a few unique holidays and events that can be celebrated in class or at home to promote diversity, support literacy, and show appreciation for dual-language children.

- Celebrating the Bilingual Child Month (October)
- Multicultural Children's Book Day (last Friday in January)
- World Folktales and Fables Week (third week of March)
- National Reading Month (March)
- Children's Day (second Sunday of June)
- World Refugee Day (June 20)
- Giving Tuesday (Tuesday after U.S. Thanksgiving)

This section provides more information about these special events, and how teachers or homeschooling families can recognize and celebrate them.

Celebrating the Bilingual Child Month

Although there are many benefits to childhood bilingualism, many people do not recognize this (let alone celebrate it). *Celebrating the Bilingual Child Month* in October was established specifically to recognize and show appreciation for bilingual children.

Having a month set aside each year to celebrate childhood bilingualism is a wonderful way to instill pride in bilingual children and involve bilingual families in classroom activities. Due to the importance of *Celebrating the Bilingual Child Month* in a diverse, multilingual classroom, this section includes 10 ways to recognize this event. Section 4 also includes a handout about celebrating this event that can be shared or posted.

There are many ways for teachers to celebrate bilingual children in the classroom. Below are just 10 ideas to help celebrate this month in a special way:

1. Recognize bilingual children in class

Ask bilingual children in class to share a bit about their languages and cultures. Don't embarrass them if they are shy. Instead, help them to feel excited and proud of their linguistic and cultural heritage.

2. Invite parents to read bilingual books out loud

Ask the parents of immigrant students if they would be willing to come to class at a set time to help read a bilingual book out loud to the students. The parent can read one sentence or page in his or her language and the teacher can read the same sentence or page in English. There are so many ways to make this interactive and fun for both the parents and the students.

3. Highlight children in other countries

Find some videos of children doing everyday tasks in their home countries. For example, videos of children going to school, helping around the house, going shopping with family, and playing games can be especially insightful for students in your class.

4. Show different alphabets

Many students have no idea that some languages are written with different letters, written scripts, and characters. Educators can learn how to pronounce a few words in different alphabets and scripts so that they can share them with students. Discuss the similarities and differences. Even better, help children write a few Chinese characters or Arabic words. Children can spend many days focused on how to write letters and words in different alphabets, and teachers can invite a bilingual parent to help out. *(Note: The language profiles in this book can be used to give background information about different languages. In addition, a lesson available for free download includes an activity on children creating their own languages using symbols. See Section 4 for more information on the lesson plan downloads.)*

5. Discuss how it feels to *not* understand

Invite a parent or someone from the community to talk with students about what it feels like to *not* be able to understand what others are saying. Have this person then speak to students in his or her language and ask the students direct questions in the language, using a lot of expression and a variety of voice levels. Have this go on long enough so that the students get a real sense of what it feels like to not understand what someone is saying. Afterward, talk with the students about how they felt and write down these feelings on the board. This list can be used all month in a variety of subjects and activities.

6. Have parents bring in traditional foods

There is nothing more fun than trying foods from different countries. Ask parents if they can bring some of their traditional foods and have a potluck. Have the parents briefly introduce each of their foods at the potluck so that other participants can learn something about each dish. Make sure to have fun with this event and allow children to say what they really think of each food in a respectful way.

7. Send home information

Create single pages that discuss the benefits of bilingualism and send one of these pages home each week with the students. The information might be links to articles online or a synopsis of research about bilingualism. Parents are delighted to be informed about things like this. Just make sure not to overwhelm them with too much information. *(Feel free to share articles from the Language Lizard Blog and those listed in Section 4 of this book.)*

8. Share traditional clothing and items

Ask the bilingual children in class to bring in some traditional items from their home countries that they can share with the other students. Explain to students what "traditional" means and then ask the rest of the students to tell about items that they have at home which are traditional to their family and culture.

9. Bring bilingual books home

Each week talk about a different language in class and then give your students a bilingual book with this language to take home to share with family members. Students feel empowered by their knowledge and cultural awareness when they can share it with others, especially family. Parents can read portions of the book in English and talk with their children about words in the other language that are similar and different.

10. Throw a party

Children remember things that involve planning, fun, and celebration. One of the best ways to enjoy *Celebrating The Bilingual Child Month* is with a real, live party. Have balloons, music from different cultures in different languages, and games. There is no need to make everything specifically about languages and cultures. Just have fun. But make sure children know that the reason for the party is to celebrate the wonders and joys of bilingualism.

The best part about childhood bilingualism is that if children start learning languages at a young age, they will have a whole lifetime to experiences to perfect them. Languages learned in childhood become part of who they are. Growing up bilingual gives a child the chance to be part of a global experience even before he or she comes to realize that the world is as big and expansive as it is.

While the suggestions outlined above are important activities for the entire year, *Celebrating the Bilingual Child Month* provides a special opportunity to highlight the wonderful aspects of bilingualism and multiculturalism. Encourage teachers and families to expose children and students to languages as often as possible, even without a set plan and curriculum. Learning a few words in another language, seeing another written script in a bilingual book, and hearing another language spoken for a few minutes can open up a child's world in ways that we cannot even begin to measure.

Multicultural Children's Book Day

The last Friday in January is *Multicultural Children's Book Day*. It is a day to "not only raise awareness for the kid's books that celebrate diversity, but to get more of these books into classrooms and libraries."

To recognize this special day, readers can use #ReadYourWorld on social media, and share their love of diverse characters and multicultural stories. It is an easy way to help get more multicultural children's books out into the world. Readers can go to the event's website (*www.multiculturalchildrensbookday.com*) to download resources such as diversity activities, book lists, and more.

Multicultural books allow children to see themselves in the stories. Until very recently, the vast majority of characters in children's books in the U.S. were white, in spite of the fact that by 2020, more than half of American children will identify as a non-white ethnicity.

It can be disheartening for students to read a never-ending stream of stories featuring characters they do not relate to. Students get a boost of self-esteem when they read or hear books in which their cultures or ethnicities are represented and celebrated.

In addition, multicultural books help children to see life through another person's eyes. This builds empathy - understanding, respecting, and placing value on another person's perspective. Children's books are a great way to introduce an entirely new point of view, show a different way of life, and address important life topics.

World Folktales and Fables Week

World Folktales and Fables Week is the third week of March and is a great opportunity to enjoy a good folktale in the classroom or home.

Reading world folktales and fables is not only a wonderful way to entertain children, it is also an effective way to educate them. The stories in classic folklore offer both social lessons as well as an opportunity to teach about cultures and languages.

Children love folktales and fables. With their simple characters and settings, as well as an enticing conflict early in the story, folktales immediately grab a reader's attention. Recall *The Three Billy Goats Gruff*, in which all three goats need to get to the other side of the bridge for food, but a hungry troll stands in their way. The stories develop quickly, and often obstacles seem insurmountable but, in the end, everything is resolved to our satisfaction. Good triumphs over evil.

The repetition and rhythm we see in stories such as *Goldilocks and the Three Bears* and *The Little Red Hen and the Grains of Wheat*, are also very appealing to children. And, of course, everyone loves when humor and cunning are used to outsmart an adversary. Folktales provide an excellent way to teach children about the consequences of good and bad behavior, the importance of cooperation, and the rewards of courage and ingenuity. In *The Giant Turnip* (an adaptation of the Russian story *The Enormous Turnip)*, a class grows a huge turnip and works together to figure out how to pull it out of the ground. The story helps young children grasp the benefits of community and working together.

Folktales also offer a great entry point for teaching children about other cultures. For instance, the fable *Dragon's Tears* is a wonderful starting point to explore Chinese Culture. *Ali Baba and the Forty Thieves* can be used to begin teaching and learning about Arabic culture.

Bilingual editions of these traditional stories allow the parent or teacher to expose children not only to a different culture, but also to another language. For instance, the bilingual version of the Indian folktale *Buri and the Marrow* introduces children to traditional Indian stories and foreign language scripts.

Folktales and fables have survived the test of time for a reason. This special week is a good time to pick up a story, sit down with a child, and enjoy. The folktales and lesson plans in Section 2 of this book offer a great place to start.

National Reading Month

Every March, *National Reading Month* kicks off with the National Education Association's *Read Across America Day*, which celebrates the birthday of the beloved Dr. Seuss. All month long, organizations across the country hold events that celebrate the love of reading, and encourage children and adults to enjoy new books or revisit old favorites. This is a great time to try out new multicultural books with young children and celebrate with fun books that introduce them to different cultures.

Children's Day

Every June, *Children's Day* is celebrated in more than 50 countries around the world. Generally, it is a day to celebrate the happiness and growth of children, and commit to protecting their well- being. In the U.S., *Children's Day* is the second Sunday of June. While the holiday is not widely celebrated in the U.S., there is a movement to bring more attention to the holiday, and increase its popularity.

Although the customs vary in each country, *Children's Day* is usually celebrated with fruit juices, child-friendly treats, and fun decorations, like dolls and streamers. It is a good time to teach children about kids around the world.

World Refugee Day

World Refugee Day on June 20th is marked in over 100 countries. Its goal is to raise awareness and funds to help provide refugees with shelter, food, and safety.

More than half of the world's refugees are children. Refugee children in the U.S. face many challenges when adapting to a new life: culture shock, making friends, and learning a new language are just a few. This day is a good time to offer age-appropriate lessons about refugees. In addition, consider opportunities to engage in fundraising to support a refugee assistance organization.

Please see Section 4 for educational resources to help ease the transition for refugees and other newcomers.

Giving Tuesday

Giving Tuesday (#GivingTuesday) was founded by New York's 92nd Street Y, in partnership with the United Nations Foundation, as a global movement involving numerous organizations. Falling the Tuesday after Thanksgiving (in the U.S.), this movement helps to shift the focus from the shopping that occurs heavily on the Friday and Monday after Thanksgiving toward charitable giving. It is a global day dedicated to giving back.

This time of year presents a perfect opportunity to discuss areas around the world (or in students' own communities) that could use support. It is also a great time to brainstorm about how students can help children in need.

ADDITIONAL RESOURCES

"We should all know that diversity makes for a rich tapestry, and we must understand that all the threads of the tapestry are equal in value no matter what their color."
- Maya Angelou

This section provides a list of resources that will help educators support immigrant children, refugees, and bilingual families. In addition to links to various resources, we have provided information about free lesson plans and articles from the Language Lizard Blog that will help teachers promote bilingualism and multicultural education. New articles are added every month, so feel free to explore and share as needed.

Resources/links are offered about the following topics:

- Supporting newcomers, immigrants, and refugees
- Building a welcoming, multicultural classroom
- Promoting community in the classroom
- Encouraging parental involvement
- Supporting language development
- Useful data resources
- Free multicultural lesson plans

At the end of this section, we have also included special handouts:

- "HELLO" in different languages - handout and reference sheet
- "I'm Bilingual, What's Your Superpower?" activity sheet
- A one-page handout for *Celebrating the Bilingual Child Month*.

The "HELLO" in different languages page is a great handout for the first day of class to get children to learn a little bit about diverse languages. They can also welcome each other and find out more about the different languages spoken by their classmates. Feel free to add any languages to the handout.

The "I'm Bilingual, What's Your Superpower?" activity sheet provides a fun way for bilingual children to share more information about themselves.

The *Celebrating the Bilingual Child Month* handout is a nice item to share with other teachers in the beginning of the school year to come up with a plan for how to recognize and celebrate the diversity in the school and community.

Resources/Links

Supporting Newcomers, Immigrants, and Refugees

English Learner Tool Kit (Office of English Language Acquisition, U.S. Department of Education)
https://www2.ed.gov/about/offices/list/oela/english-learner-toolkit/index.html

Resources for Immigrants, Refugees, Asylees and Other New Americans (U.S. Department of Education)
https://www2.ed.gov/about/overview/focus/immigration-resources.html

How to Help Students Survive Culture Shock
https://blog.languagelizard.com/2012/02/23/how-to-help-students-survive-culture-shock/

Immigrant and Refugee Children: A Guide for Educators and School Support Staff (The American Federation of Teachers)
https://www.aft.org/sites/default/files/im_uac-educators-guide_2016.pdf

Refugee Children in U.S. Schools: A Toolkit for Teachers and School Personnel (BRYCS - Bridging Refugee Youth & Children's Services)
https://brycs.org/toolkit/refugee-children-in-u-s-schools-a-toolkit-for-teachers-and-school-personnel/

How to Support Refugee Students in the ELL Classroom (Colorin Colorado)
https://www.colorincolorado.org/article/how-support-refugee-students-ell-classroom

Building a Welcoming Multicultural Classroom

Strategies for Supporting All Dual Language Learners (National Center on Cultural and Linguistic Responsiveness)
https://eclkc.ohs.acf.hhs.gov/sites/default/files/pdf/dll-strategies.pdf

Welcoming Refugee Students: Strategies for Classroom Teachers (NY Bureau of Refugee and Immigrant Assistance)
https://otda.ny.gov/programs/bria/documents/WtOS-Strategies-for-Teachers-Brochure.pdf

How to Create a Welcoming Classroom Environment (Colorin Colorado)
https://www.colorincolorado.org/article/how-create-welcoming-classroom-environment

Making Your Head Start Classroom Welcoming for Multilingual Kids
https://blog.languagelizard.com/2013/05/03/home-languages-head-start/

Building a Lending Library in Your Classroom
https://blog.languagelizard.com/2016/08/30/3-steps-to-build-a-lending-library-in-your-classroom/

Promoting Community in the Classroom

Effective Social and Emotional Learning Programs: Preschool and Elementary School Edition (CASEL - Collaborative for Academic, Social, and Emotional Learning)
http://casel.org/wp-content/uploads/2016/01/2013-casel-guide-1.pdf

14 Ways to Cultivate Classroom Chemistry (Teaching Channel)
https://www.teachingchannel.org/blog/2012/09/10/14-ways-to-cultivate-classroom-chemistry/

Creating an Emotionally Healthy Classroom Environment (Edutopia)
https://www.edutopia.org/blog/creating-emotionally-healthy-classroom-environment-mark-phillips

Creating Community in the Classroom
https://blog.languagelizard.com/2015/08/21/creating-community-in-the-classroom-tips-free-lesson-plan-bilingual-multicultural-language/

Teaching Tolerance in Turbulent Times
https://blog.languagelizard.com/2016/07/06/teaching-tolerance-in-turbulent-times/

Encouraging Parental Involvement

Partnering with Parents and Families to Support Immigrant and Refugee Children at School (Center for Health and Health Care in Schools)
https://www.education.ne.gov/wp-content/uploads/2017/07/Partnering-with-Parents-and-Families-To-Support-Immigrant-and-Refugee-Children-at-School.pdf

Tools and Resources for Ensuring Meaningful Communication with Limited English Proficient Parents (Department of Education)
https://www2.ed.gov/about/offices/list/oela/english-learner-toolkit/chap10.pdf

Benefits of Home Language Maintenance, From Parents' Perspectives
https://blog.languagelizard.com/2017/12/06/benefits-of-home-language-maintenance-from-parents-perspectives/

Home Language Maintenance Strategies
https://blog.languagelizard.com/2018/03/20/home-language-maintenance-strategies/

Supporting Language Development

Bilingual Students: Using Holiday Celebrations to Promote Language Development in Multicultural Classrooms
https://blog.languagelizard.com/2013/01/10/bilingual-students-holiday-celebrations-language-development-multicultural-classrooms/

Supporting Oral Language Development in the Classroom & At Home
https://blog.languagelizard.com/2016/05/11/supporting-oral-language-development-in-the-classroom-at-home/

Challenging Common Myths About Young English Language Learners (Foundation for Child Development)
https://www.fcd-us.org/assets/2016/04/MythsOfTeachingELLsEspinosa.pdf

Useful Data Resources

Readers can learn more about the diversity in a particular community using the Modern Language Association's Language Map. Users can find the number of speakers of each foreign language by zip code, city, county or state at the following link: https://apps.mla.org/map_main

The information is also available from the U.S. Census Bureau:
https://www.census.gov/
https://factfinder.census.gov/

Kids Count Data Center (Annie E. Casey Foundation)
https://datacenter.kidscount.org

Migration Policy Institute Immigration Data
https://www.Migrationpolicy.org/datamatters

MPI Dual Language Learners Report
https://www.migrationpolicy.org/research/dual-language-learners-national-demographic-and-policy-profile

Free Multicultural Lesson Plans

This book contains eleven multicultural lesson plans, but Language Lizard offers many more free lessons online representing different countries, cultures, and topics. Lessons include:

- International Holidays
- Understanding and Appreciating Cultural Differences
- Building Community in the Classroom
- Appreciating Diverse Cultures and Religions

Lesson plans can be accessed at the following link: https://www.languagelizard.com/Multicultural-Lessons

Greet Your Neighbors
Hello in Different Languages
Handout and Language Key

To download a printable version of the "Hello" chart, please visit www.languagelizard.com/Bonus.

Language Guide for Hello in Different Languages Handout:

Hello (English)	Merhaba (Turkish)
Ni hao (Mandarin Chinese)	Néih hóu (Cantonese Chinese)
Hola (Spanish)	Privet (Russian)
Bonjour (French)	Hej (Swedish, Danish)
Konnichiwa (Japanese)	Oi (Portuguese - Brazilian)
Vanakkam (Tamil)	Salut (Romanian)
Marhaban (Arabic)	Annyeong haseyo (Korean)
Guten tag (German)	Namaskar (Punjabi)
Min-ga-la-ba (Burmese)	Cześć (Polish)
Olá (Portuguese)	Musta (Tagalog)
Namaste (Hindi, Gujarati, Malayalam, Nepali)	Salām (Urdu)
Salaam (Farsi, Pashto)	Ẹ n lẹ (Yoruba)
O-si-yo (Cherokee)	Hallo (Dutch)
Shalom (Hebrew)	Hujambo (Swahili)
Ciao (Italian)	Chào (Vietnamese)
Nomoskaar (Bengali)	Vanakka (Tamil)
	Sillaw (Kurdish - Sorani)

I'm Bilingual, What's Your Superpower? Activity Sheet

To receive a printable version of this handout, please visit www.LanguageLizard.com/
Bonus.

I'M BILINGUAL WHAT'S YOUR ← ≪ SUPERPOWER?

I SPEAK THESE LANGUAGES: _____
_____
MY FAMILY COMES FROM: _____
_____
MY FAVORITE HOLIDAYS ARE: _____
_____
MY HOBBIES ARE: _____
_____
THIS IS A BOOK I REALLY LIKE: _____
_____
HERE'S MORE INFORMATION ABOUT ME: _____
_____
_____
_____

Celebrating the Bilingual Child Month (October) Teacher Suggestions Handout

To receive a printable version of this document, please visit www.LanguageLizard.com/Bonus.

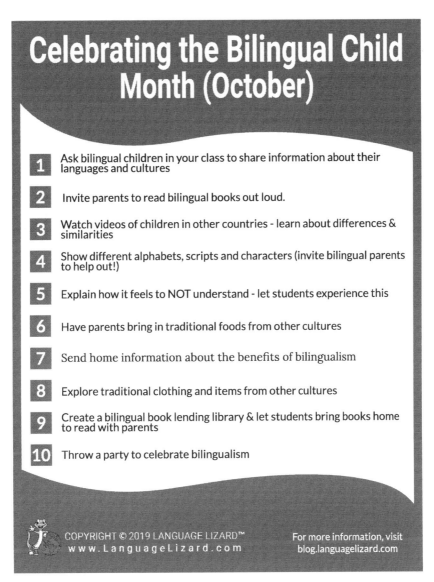

Read more about each of these 10 suggestions at the following link: https://blog.languagelizard.com/2011/10/08/celebrate-the-bilingual-children-month/

RESOURCES and IMAGES

Resources

Adair, Jennifer. (September, 2015) *"The Impact of Discrimination on the Early Schooling Experiences of Children from Immigrant Families."* Migration Policy Institute Reports, https://www.migrationpolicy.org/research/impact-discrimination-early-schooling-experiences-children-immigrant-families.

Bear, D. R., Invernizzi, M., Templeton, S., & Johnston, F. (2016). *Words Their Way: Word Study for Phonics, Vocabulary, and Spelling Instruction* (6th ed.). Upper Saddle River, NJ: Prentice Hall.

Barbarash, L. (1997). *Multicultural Games*. Champaign, IL: Human Kinetics.

Culture. In *Merriem-Webster*. Retrieved from https://www.merriem-webster.com/dictionary/culture

Cummins, J., Bismilla, V., Chow, P., Cohen, S., Giampapa, F., Leoni, L.,...Sastri, P. (2005). Affirming Identity in Multilingual Classrooms. *Educational Leadership*, 38-43.

Davies Samway, K. & McKeon, D. (2002). Myths about acquiring a second language. In Power, B.M., & Hubbard, R.S. (Eds.) *Language Development a Reader for Teachers* (2nd Ed.), (pp.62-68).Upper Saddle River, NJ: Merrill Prentice Hall.

Ganske. K. *Word Journey: Assessment Guided Phonics, Spelling, and Vocabulary Instruction*. (2000). New York, NY: The Guilford Press.

Gillanders, C., Castro, D.C., & Franco, X. (2014). Learning words for life: Promoting vocabulary in dual language learners. *The Reading Teacher, 68*(3), 213-221. DOI: 10.1002/trtr.1291.

Li, G. (2008). Parenting practices and schooling: The way class works for new immigrant groups. In Weis, L. (Ed.), *The way class works: Readings on school, family, and the economy* (pp.149-166). New York, NY: Routledge Taylor & Francis Group.

Nagi, W. (2005). Why vocabulary instruction needs to be long-term and comprehensive. In E. H. Hiebert & M.L. Kamil (Eds.), *Teaching and learning vocabulary: Bringing research to practice* (27-44). Mahwah, NJ: Lawerence Elbaum.

Naqvi, R., McKeough, A., Thorne, K., & Pfitscher, C. (2013). Dual-language books as an emergent-literacy resource: Culturally and linguistically responsive teaching and learning. *Journal of Early Childhood Literacy*, *13*(4), 501-528.

Sims Bishop, R. (1990). Mirrors, windows, and sliding glass doors. *Perspectives*, *6*(3), 9-12.

Sneddon, R. (2008). Young bilingual children learning to read with dual language books. *English Teaching*, *7*(2), 71.

Sneddon, R. (2009). *Bilingual books: biliterate children learning to read through dual language books*. Sterling, VA: Trentham Books Ltd.

U.S. Census Bureau. (2016). American Community Surveys.

U.S. Census Bureau. (2017). Current Population Survey.

Book Images

Introduction (book covers)

Ali Baba and the Forty Thieves (2005) by Enebor Attard, illustrated by Richard Holland
Goal! Let's Play! (2009) by Joe Marriott, illustrated by Algy Craig Hall
Mungo Makes New Friends (2018) by Gill Aitchison, illustrated by Jill Newton
Grandma's Saturday Soup (2005) by Sally Fraser, illustrated by Derek Brazell
Let's Go to the Park (2016) by Kate Clynes, illustrated by Sarah Mills

Section 2 (book covers)

Welcome to the World Baby (2005) by Na'ima bint Robert, illustrated by Derek Brazell.
The Wibbly Wobbly Tooth (2003) by David Mills, illustrated by Julia Crouth.- *Mei Ling's Hiccups* (2000) by David Mills, illustrated by Derek Brazell
The Giant Turnip (2001) by Henriette Barkow, illustrated by Richard Johnson
The Children of Lir (2003) by Dawn Casey, illustrated by Diana Mayo
Yeh-Hsien a Chinese Cinderella (2006) by Dawn Casey, illustrated by Richard Holland
Li's Chinese New Year (2010) by Fang Wang, illustrated by Jennifer Corfield.
Samira's Eid (1999) by Nasreen Aktar, illustrated by Enebor Attard
Deepak's Diwali (2009) by Divya Karwal, illustrated by Doreen Lang
Marek and Alice's Christmas (2008) by Jolanta Starek-Corile, illustrations by Priscilla Lamont.

Section 3 (book pages)

Arabic: *Alfie's Angels* (2003) by Henriette Barkow, illustrated by Sarah Garson.

Chinese: *Yeh-Hsien a Chinese Cinderella* (2006) by Dawn Casey, illustrated by Richard Holland.

Farsi: *Goose Fables* (2010) by Shaun Chatto, illustrated by Jago

French: *Buri and the Marrow* (2000) by Henriette Barkow, illustrated by Lizzie Finlay

German: *Don't Cry Sly* (2002) by Henriette Barkow, illustrated by Richard Johnson

Hindi: *Ali Baba and the Forty Thieves* (2005) by Enebor Attard, illustrated by Richard Holland

Japanese: *Fox Fables* (2006) by Dan Casey, illustrated by Jago

Nepali: *Keeping Up With Cheetah* (1993; dual language edition 2008) by Lindsay Camp, illustrated by Jill Newton

Russian: *Sports Day in the Jungle* (2010) by Jill Newton, illustrated by Jill Newton

Somali: *The Elves and the Shoemaker* (2007) by Henriette Barkow, illustrated by Jago

Spanish: *Pandora's Box* (2002) by Henriette Barkow, illustrated by Diana Mayo

Thanks to Mishti Chatterji of Mantra Lingua for permission to reproduce cover illustrations and page images.

ABOUT THE AUTHORS

Anneke Forzani is the President and Founder of *Language Lizard LLC*, which supplies schools, libraries, and literacy organizations with multicultural resources in over 50 languages. As a first generation American, Anneke always loved learning foreign languages and studying other cultures. She learned Dutch, French, and Japanese and worked in several multicultural and international business positions in the U.S. and Japan. Anneke ultimately chose to devote herself to promoting literacy and multicultural education to help build a generation of culturally aware and understanding global citizens. Anneke has presented workshops about using multicultural resources in diverse classrooms at educational conferences. She is the author of the forthcoming children's books, *Happy After All* and *Juan's Stone Soup*. Anneke lives in Basking Ridge, NJ and enjoys hiking, cycling, and skiing with her husband and four sons.

Dr. Heather Leaman works with pre-service teachers focusing on social studies in the elementary grades. She also works with practicing teachers in the Master's of Education program at West Chester University, and coordinates their M.Ed program in Applied Studies in Teaching and Learning, supporting teachers as they conduct classroom-based research. Prior to this, Dr. Leaman spent 11 years teaching sixth grade in a Pennsylvania public school. Dr. Leaman's initial interest in using bilingual resources emerged during her work with middle school students who brought rich language and cultural diversity to the school where she worked.

Edmond Gubbins and Ellen O'Regan both teach elementary school in Ireland. They have Bachelor of Education degrees from Mary Immaculate College in Limerick, Ireland, and Master's of Education degrees from West Chester University in Pennsylvania. They have a keen interest in multiculturalism and fostering an appreciation for diversity in their students.

*Dear Reader - This book was a labor of love. It was born from a desire to support language learners, immigrants, and refugees in the midst of challenging societal changes. I hope this book will support your efforts to raise culturally aware global citizens. If you like what you read, **please leave a review** on Amazon, Goodreads, or other online platforms. Your help will allow Language Lizard to continue to offer free multicultural lesson plans on our site. Thank you!*

BONUS FOR READERS

Download More Multicultural Lesson Plans and Free Resources for Diverse Classrooms!

www.LanguageLizard.com/Bonus

There are many more lesson plans available on the Language Lizard site, covering diverse regions, languages and topics. Subjects include:

- Understanding and Appreciating Cultural Differences
- Building Community in the Classroom
- Appreciating Diverse Cultures and Religions
- Supporting our Classmates: Folktales, Bullying, and Problem Solving
- Language, Customs, and Culture in Countries Around the World
- Happiness (Social & Emotional Well-being)

You will also receive downloadable versions of the following three charts:

- A colorful *Greet Your Neighbors* chart with "Hello" in many languages
- "I'm Bilingual, What's Your Superpower?" activity sheet
- "Celebrating the Bilingual Child Month" - teacher suggestions handout

Plus... receive a special discount on the multicultural/bilingual books featured in the lesson plans in this book.

Access the lesson plans and other special offers now at:
www.LanguageLizard.com/Bonus

Made in the USA
Middletown, DE
01 December 2019